RESCUING
RETIREMENT

RESCUING
RETIREMENT

A Plan to Guarantee
Retirement Security
for All Americans

TONY JAMES *and*
TERESA GHILARDUCCI

**DISRUPTION
BOOKS**

Austin   New York

Published by Disruption Books
Austin, TX and New York, NY
www.disruptionbooks.com

Distributed by Disruption Books

For ordering information or special discounts for bulk purchases, please contact Disruption Books at info@disruptionbooks.com.

Cover design, text design, and composition by Kim Lance

Print ISBN: 978-1-63331-009-4
eBook ISBN: 978-1-63331-010-0

First Edition

To our children
Joseph, Meredith, Becky, and Ham

And to all the retirees of tomorrow,
who are entitled to retire with dignity

Our plan would guarantee millions of Americans safe and secure retirements that would benefit them, their families, and the nation's economy.

—The New York Times, *2016*[1]

Contents

America's Broken Retirement System

A Problem We Can Solve, a Disaster If We Don't

$14,500	The average retirement savings balance of an American between the ages of 40 and 55.
$18,433	The median savings in an American 401(k) account.[2]
$375,000	The approximate amount the average American needs to save to retire comfortably.
10,000	The number of Americans retiring every single day.
25 million	The number of retired Americans who will face poverty or near-poverty in retirement by the year 2050.

62%	The percentage of private sector workers with retirement plans participating exclusively in traditional defined benefit pension retirement plans in 1979.
7%	The percentage who do today.[3]
68%	The percentage of the working age population (25–64) who currently don't have an employer retirement plan—either because their employer does not offer one, they don't participate, or they are not working. [4]
55%	The percentage of households near retirement age who will have to subsist almost entirely on Social Security income. [5]
86%	The percentage of Americans who believe America "faces a retirement crisis."
84%	The percentage of Americans who want "national policymakers to give more attention to retirement issues."

This is a crisis, but it's a crisis we can solve.
A better, stronger, more secure retirement future is
possible. In the pages ahead, we'll explain how.

Foreword

Bill Jasien

FOR OVER TWENTY YEARS, I'VE WORKED WITHIN AMERICA'S retirement system. I've watched it evolve. I've seen it fracture. And I realize now more than ever that it needs a revolutionary change.

That's why I'm so glad that two leading industry experts, Teresa Ghilarducci and Tony James, have addressed the retirement challenge head-on. We may disagree on many political issues, but regardless of one's political alignment, aspects of Teresa and Tony's Retirement Savings Plan provide an important road map to put American workers back on track toward achieving their retirement objectives.

It's a plan that recognizes a simple fact: Much of the retirement planning infrastructure in this country was haphazardly constructed. Today it is so antiquated that it fails to meet the needs of millions of people across the United States. And that problem will only get worse in the years to come.

In large part, this arises directly from a massive change that began in 1980. That was the year traditional defined benefit (DB) pension plans started going out of style—and more and more private employers began offering defined contribution (DC) plans like 401(k)s instead. It's important to note that, initially, DC plans were simply meant to offer individuals the opportunity to build an additional retirement nest egg on a voluntary basis. Indeed, because these plans require individuals to manage their own investment strategies, they are actually much less effective. For many reasons and unfortunately, the typical person managing his or her own DC plan earns just about half of the returns he or she could expect from a professionally managed pension plan.

When these DC plans began rolling out more than three decades ago, the vast majority of workers with retirement plans were still covered with some form of a traditional defined benefit pension. In part due to the advent of these DC plans, however, a major restructuring of America's retirement system commenced.

Defined benefit plans may be great for employees, but for employers, they are expensive, with high contingent liabilities. Defined contribution plans, by contrast, effectively transferred the entire risk of and responsibility for retirement from employers to employees.

With this in mind, many employers began to restructure their DB plans—or terminate them entirely—using the new, much less expensive DC plans as convenient substitutions. Before long, the stable retirement safety net deteriorated considerably; in its place were the often dramatically underfunded and poorly managed personal DC plans, combined with a Social Security system ill-equipped to shoulder the increasing retirement burden.

As a result, America's retirees are now facing an income replacement crisis that, if not addressed aggressively, will have serious social and economic consequences for our country. For the next twenty years or so, about 10,000 Americans will turn 65 each day—and most of them won't have nearly the savings needed to replace an adequate portion of their income and thereby maintain their standard of living in retirement.

This is why Teresa and Tony's plan is so important. It articulates how some of the positive attributes of defined benefit plans can be incorporated within a personal retirement savings plan. That way, one can adopt the positive aspects of a DB structure that secured a stable retirement for generations—but without the expensive, long-term contingent liabilities.

Tony and Teresa also recognize that a comfortable retirement spanning decades can be achieved much more effectively through prudent, consistent investment by individuals in our free market economy. This enables each worker to benefit from the power of compounded returns. And crucially, their plan is built on commonsense principles, key to advancing the debate on a bipartisan basis.

Teresa and Tony's plan provides a bold, fresh approach to modernizing America's retirement infrastructure. As a country, we have a choice: We can continue to nibble around the edges, pretending the problem will magically heal itself; or we can engage in a spirited debate for a responsible, innovative, and efficient model that will meet the needs of future generations and likely head off a social and economic crisis for our country.

As a board member of the Federal Retirement Thrift Investment Board (FRTIB), Bill Jasien helps oversee the largest retirement system in America, with 4.8 million participants and $450 billion in assets. For over twenty years he has served at the highest levels of business and government, including a tour as President George H. W. Bush's deputy assistant secretary of the US Treasury. Today he is the CEO of StoneHedge Global Partners and the executive chairman of the National Association of Counties Financial Services Corporation, an organization focused on aggregating solutions, including retirement and health care, for the benefit of local governmental entities.

Society's Coming Retirement Crisis

ROBERT HILTONSMITH CAPTURES SO MUCH OF WHAT'S wrong with our retirement system. He is an economist in his mid-30s. Given his career and his relative youth, he should have all the tools he needs to plan for a comfortable retirement.

But when PBS's *Frontline* interviewed him for a special on the American retirement system, his outlook couldn't have been more pessimistic or revealing.

"My retirement plan is 'fingers crossed and pray,' basically. Yeah, win the lottery, hope my dad has more money than he does," Hiltonsmith said. "The truth is, [I'm] just going to have to find a way to save way more than you should have to."[6]

Right now, America's retirement system is so hopelessly broken—and so ruthlessly confusing for the average worker—that even Americans who work consistent well-compensated full-time jobs for their entire adult lives find it difficult to guarantee a comfortable retirement.

Many more workers, especially those who work in lower-compensated positions, face an even more daunting challenge. Without significant savings, they are forced to try to continue

Young Workers Say They're Worried About Retirement

What is a "significant source of stress" in your life?

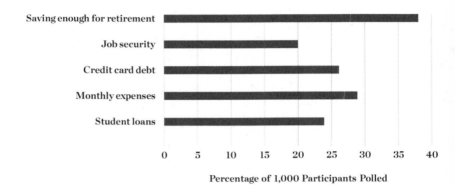

Percentage of 1,000 Participants Polled

Source: Schwab Retirement Plan Services, Inc. (August 2016) 401(k) Participant Survey.

working until the very end of their lives, well aware that a single health crisis or accident could send them spiraling into poverty.

America stands at a critical moment. The issue of retirement security is gaining attention at a time when more Americans than ever are approaching retirement with inadequate savings. That number is set to increase dramatically in the coming years, and these Americans are living longer, too. Since 1980, the number of Americans living past age 90 has tripled—meaning retirement savings need to last longer than ever.[7]

Even as life expectancies rise, however, the retirement savings tools offered—mostly 401(k)s and IRAs—are deeply inadequate. They are badly designed, accumulating insufficient savings and earning investment returns that are much too low. In fact, among Americans lucky enough to have access to 401(k) plans, less than 50 percent actually have enough to retire. When you look at the broader population of Americans between the ages of 40 and 55, the average retirement account balance is just $14,500.[8] That's a fraction of what the average worker needs for retirement—about $400,000 in savings.[9]

For the next generation of retirees—today's young people—the challenges are even greater. Entry-level wages are stagnant; health, rent, and child-care costs are escalating; outstanding student loan debt remains above $1 trillion. They face productivity and economic growth rates in the next 50 years equal to only half of what we enjoyed in the last 50 years. At the same time, near-zero interest rates around the world have pulled down the returns Americans can expect to earn on any savings they do manage to put aside.

Given this stark reality, it's little wonder that a 2015 survey found that 86 percent of Americans "believe that the nation faces a retirement crisis."[10]

Indeed, if current trends continue, we will soon face rates of poverty among senior citizens not seen since the Great Depression. Of the 18 million workers who were between the ages of 55 and 64 in 2012, 4.3 million will be poor or near-poor when they turn 65 years old.[11] This number will include 2.6 million workers who were part of the middle class before reaching retirement age. By 2035 there will be nearly 20 million retirees living in poverty or near-poverty—and by 2050 that number will reach 25 million.

So numerous are those facing poverty that, if they made up a state, it would surpass Florida as the third most populous state in America. A wave of older poor Americans of this magnitude will strain social safety net programs from food stamps to Medicaid—and will devastate federal, state, and local budgets for decades.

The expenses of older Americans living at or near the poverty level will inevitably be passed on to other citizens in other ways, too: from

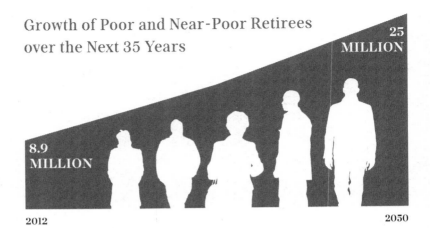

Growth of Poor and Near-Poor Retirees over the Next 35 Years

25 MILLION

8.9 MILLION

2012

2050

Source: T. Ghilarducci and Z. Knauss. (2015) "More Middle Class Workers Will Be Poor Retirees." Schwartz Center for Economic Policy Analysis and Department of Economics, The New School for Social Research, Policy Note Series.

higher insurance premiums to cover a rise in emergency room visits, to the taxpayer burden that inevitably comes with a significant spike in homelessness. One study in Utah, for instance, finds a significant increase in government spending is anticipated due to an increase in elderly poverty. We can expect similar trends across the United States.

As the retirement crisis escalates, even many of those who don't slip into actual poverty will still experience a dramatic reduction in quality of life when they reach retirement. Over half of working people near retirement right now won't have enough savings to maintain their standard of living.[12]

Our country, in other words, is facing an across-the-board retirement savings gap. Americans of almost all ages and income levels face nearly insurmountable obstacles to building a strong retirement foundation. And one way or another, it will affect us all in the years to come.

If the status quo continues, over the next 35 years, the population of retirees living in or near poverty will grow to the equivalent of the population of the shaded states.

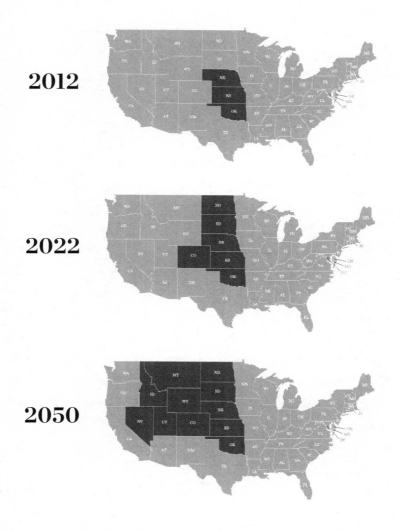

2012

2022

2050

Source: US Census Bureau (2010), "2010 Resident Population Data."

A Better Way Forward

There's a much better way forward for our country. It's a journey we can start today, drawing on straightforward, proven ideas.

It's a way to ensure every full-time worker saves enough to guarantee their standard of living in retirement.

A way to offer access to a retirement savings tool that delivers a significantly higher rate of return than a 401(k) or IRA.

A way to address a national crisis without adding a dime to the deficit or creating any new government infrastructure.

In this book, we've designed a retirement system that meets these goals. In fact, our solution is simpler than you might think.

No, it's not another plan that tries to replace Social Security. In fact, it doesn't touch Social Security at all.

That isn't because Social Security is in great shape; it's not. Eventually, we will have to shore up Social Security, and waiting will only increase the cost. It is important to ensure that this essential supplemental safety net is around for generations to come.

Our plan relieves pressure on Social Security by empowering workers to save enough for retirement through an alternate approach. We're proposing a solution that makes it easier for employers and employees alike to plan for retirement in a practical, low-cost, and effective way.

All Americans stand to benefit from a smart, fiscally sound retirement system—one that's built on personal responsibility, facilitates personal savings, and guarantees that all full-time workers can be secure in their retirement. That's why we wrote this book.

Many other countries have already tackled this problem successfully, and our plan leverages the most effective elements of those systems. It empowers individual savings and lifetime retirement benefits, while bringing together ideas that both parties can support: government-backed accounts under individual control that don't impact the budget, raise taxes, or create new government bureaucracy.

It's called the *Retirement Savings Plan*—a national retirement system so simple that it could be enacted tomorrow.

———————

This proposal is the result of an unlikely pairing.

Tony is the President and Chief Operating Officer of one of the world's leading investment firms. In his work, he's seen firsthand how 401(k)s perform in the market—and how, by their very design, they're invested in ways that consistently underdeliver. This squandered return leaves the vast majority of senior citizens without enough to get by in retirement.

Teresa is a leading academic and an expert in retirement economics. She has spent decades chronicling the impact on America as retirement planning has shifted from employers to employees—many of whom are completely unprepared to meet their retirement needs. That research has revealed why even Americans who do their utmost to save for the future often still wind up retiring in poverty.

Together, we share the belief that we need to change course—and soon—to avoid an American retirement catastrophe. This book explores how the *Retirement Savings Plan* would work—explaining how it would address crucial problems in the current retirement system, answering key questions, bringing in relevant case studies, and exploring the current prospects for legislative action.

First, though, we begin with an exploration of the current retirement system, and how it has set the country on a path to crisis.

What the Retirement Savings Plan Is

Pragmatism, not politics

It is a pragmatic solution to ensure that all workers can save enough to retire. The Plan shifts our retirement system away from the current inefficient patchwork of programs and policies and toward a single, sustainable, high-performing, and pro-growth framework. It's built for bipartisanship, drawing on the best ideas from both parties.

A universal retirement solution

It is a plan that offers everyone—from Uber drivers to CEOs—their own Guaranteed Retirement Account (GRA) managed by professional portfolio managers.

A helping hand, not a handout

It is a personal savings plan, not a handout. The Plan relies on individually owned retirement accounts and existing government infrastructure to deliver results.

A plan that keeps you in control

It is built on personal responsibility, personal choice, private ownership, and effective investment. You accumulate your money in your own account, where you have full control. If you die before retirement, your savings are passed on to your spouse.

Security for life

It is lifelong retirement security. Annuitized returns ensure post-retirement income and a consistent standard of living for as long as retirees live.

A mandated gift

It is mandatory—but cost-neutral for employees earning less than America's median salary. The Plan creates a refundable $600 tax credit for every worker who contributes to their GRA. This means that households earning up to $40,000 per year will have their yearly retirement savings fully reimbursed. Higher-earning individuals will also be able to deduct the remainder of their 1.5% contribution from their taxes.

What the Retirement Savings Plan Is Not

It is not another form of Social Security.

This is your own money in your own account. The government can't ever get at the money. Each individual will buy their own annuity with their accumulated retirement savings. What's more, this plan doesn't touch Social Security as it currently exists.

It is not another new government bureaucracy.

The Retirement Savings Plan utilizes existing government infrastructure simply to make annuity payments.

It is not another program run by the government.

You contribute to a pooled trust managed by an entity of your choosing, so the returns are higher and fees lower than in an individually directed account. You decide when to retire and convert your savings into lifelong income.

It includes no new taxes, and it will not increase the deficit.

The plan's tax credits are fully paid for by redirecting existing government subsidies away from the wealthiest Americans and spreading it over the entire income distribution. In addition, by tackling the retirement crisis head-on, the plan creates additional savings for the government in the future.

How We Got Here
America's Broken Retirement "System"

TO UNDERSTAND AND SOLVE AMERICA'S RETIREMENT CRISIS, the first critical step is recognizing that the current national retirement "system" is an inefficient and accidental patchwork of programs.

It wasn't always this way. In fact, it wasn't too long ago that retirement was simple, and most workers relied on a guaranteed pension from their employers. Indeed, as recently as 1983, nearly two-thirds of private sector workers with retirement plans had traditional pension plans administered by their employers.[13]

These plans work well for retirement planning and have long been preferred by workers, but unfortunately, most private employers have phased out the traditional pension since the 1980s. Today, only 15 percent of workers—mostly government employees—have access to these defined benefit plans.

In other words, America replaced an employer-backed retirement guarantee with a system that tells savers they're on their own. Today, the vast majority of American workers find themselves stuck in a poorly designed system. They're cobbling together a retirement plan without the knowledge or tools to do so successfully.

Fully 45 percent of private sector workers do not have access to any form of employer retirement plan. That means they must rely only on personal savings at the same time wages have stagnated. A few turn to options like Keogh plans (tax-deferred retirement vehicles available to small businesses or the self-employed) and myRA (a government-backed retirement account that caps savings at $15,000). These function similarly to 401(k) plans but lack employer contributions and appropriate investment vehicles and annuity options.

... the vast majority of American workers find themselves stuck in a poorly designed system. They're cobbling together a retirement plan without the knowledge or tools to do so successfully.

Social Security provides baseline security, but not nearly enough. That's because Social Security was designed as a social insurance program, not something that could realistically maintain a middle-class retirement. The average monthly Social Security benefit is $1,300, which is totally insufficient to meet the baseline needs of most retirees.[14] Yet today we have reached a point where Social Security provides more than 90 percent of the income for 36 percent of current retirees. A full 24 percent of retirees rely on Social Security as their only source of income.

Roughly 53 percent of Americans are more fortunate—they can make use of 401(k)-type defined contribution plans backed by their employer. However, even when employees have access to a defined contribution plan, research shows they are not consistently saving and efficiently investing, mainly because the system has failed to facilitate effective retirement savings.

> *One recent Federal Reserve survey of people whose employers offer a retirement plan but who do not participate shows that 27 percent of them say they cannot afford to save any money. Another 18 percent are too confused by their choices, 18 percent more are not eligible to participate at all and another 16 percent have not gotten around to signing up.*[15]
>
> —The New York Times, *2016*

In addition, despite the wide usage of the 401(k), it's important to remember that the 401(k) fails to meet many workers' retirement needs. That's because it was never intended to be an omnibus retirement solution.[16] America's primary retirement vehicle, in fact, emerged largely by accident, gaining prominence as employers cut defined benefit plans over the last three decades.[17]

The Accidental Birth—and Spread—of the 401(k)

In 1980, a benefits consultant named Ted Benna was assigned to create a savings program for his employer. So he did what anyone would do in that situation: he pulled out a copy of the Internal Revenue Code.

Looking through the code, he found a little-noticed portion that gave employers special tax status for encouraging workers to save for retirement. He ran with the idea.

"Well, how about adding a match, an additional incentive?" Benna recalled thinking at the time in a later interview. "Immediately, I jumped to, 'Wow, this is a big deal!'" The section of the tax code he found? Section 401(k).[18]

Benna was right. His discovery was a big deal. And employers quickly realized that this retirement vehicle offered them an additional benefit: it shifted the burden and risk of providing for retirement from employers to employees. And employees didn't fully appreciate what they were losing. As a result, 401(k)s took off. In 1985, there were just 30,000 401(k) plans in existence. Today, there are 638,000.[19]

Not bad for a glorified tax loophole. But here's the problem: it doesn't work for most savers. Benna recently spoke out about how the 401(k) system is overwhelmingly complex for average workers without backgrounds in finance and investing, at one point going so far as to call his creation a "monster."[20]

"I knew it was going to be big," he said, "but I was certainly not anticipating that it would be the primary way that people would be accumulating money for retirement 30 plus years later."[21]

From the very beginning, savings vehicles like 401(k)s had some fundamental problems. Individual retirement savings accounts depend on voluntary individual contributions, which people may or may not make throughout their lives. That's a problem, because in order to be effective, these contributions *must* be made steadily throughout a worker's career, starting in their mid-twenties. Often, but not consistently, these contributions are matched by the employer. Just as important, 401(k)s also earn subpar returns on these insufficient savings as a result of poor investment strategies.

In short, we have a retirement crisis because the 35-year experiment with a do-it-yourself 401(k) system has failed. The voluntary, burdensome, commercial system doesn't adequately help employers and workers accumulate retirement assets, doesn't invest them long-term and securely with low fees, and doesn't arrange pensions for life. Average 401(k) participants simply will not have enough saved to maintain their standard of living in retirement.

Why 401(k)s Fail Savers

To understand why 401(k) plans so often leave workers with insufficient retirement savings, consider the most common ways they fail the savers who need them the most.

- They don't accumulate enough savings. Across America, the median 401(k) account balance is just $18,433. Less than 50 percent of 401(k) holders actually have enough to retire.

- They're not even close to universal. Forty-five percent of private sector workers don't have access to any workplace retirement plan. Among those who work at companies with fewer than 100 employees, only half have a 401(k) plan.

- They leave low-income and middle-income families behind. Families in the top 20 percent of income distribution are ten times more likely to have a retirement savings account than families in the lowest 20 percent. These affluent savers benefit from tax incentives that the majority of Americans cannot access.

- Low-income families don't have the ability to save even if they want to. Forty-seven percent of Americans couldn't come up with $400 if they needed it in case of an emergency.

- 401(k)s and IRAs are built to deliver lower returns. Because of a structural requirement for short-term investments (savers are able to withdraw from 401(k)s at any time), defined contribution portfolios deliver much lower returns—sometimes by as much as half—compared to defined benefit portfolios.

- They place the burden of saving, planning, and administering onto the worker. Workers with a 401(k) must figure out how much they need to save, how that money should be invested, and—once they reach retirement—how to manage their assets so they don't outlive their savings. This would be challenge enough for a savvy professional investor. It's an almost impossible burden for the average person—or even a famous surgeon.

- They ignore what motivates savings at the expense of those who need it most. As human beings, we're poorly wired to plan for the long term. For most families, if the choice is between replacing a leaky roof and preserving compound interest, most will choose fixing the leaky roof. That's what makes 401(k)s such poor savings vehicles. Not only are they opt-in savings systems, but they allow savers to liquidate their savings at any time in exchange for high fees.

- Yet 401(k)s are often a savers' only option. Despite workers' overwhelming preference for defined benefit pension plans, these retirement options have virtually evaporated in the private sector. Three decades ago, nearly two thirds of workers had a defined benefit pension. Today that number is just 15 percent, virtually all of whom are government workers.

Given all of these shortcomings, why is the 401(k) still the primary retirement vehicle for many Americans today? The answer is simple. A 401(k) isn't the best option; in most cases, it's the only option.

Six Key Problems

The Consequences of a
Broken Retirement System

AS A RESULT OF AMERICA'S PATCHWORK RETIREMENT "system" and increased reliance on defined contribution plans, there are now six fundamental problems plaguing our nation's retirement system.

1. Very few workers accumulate enough in savings, even if they are offered a workplace defined contribution plan.

In order to maintain your standard of living in retirement, a conservative estimate suggests you need to save enough to provide 70–85 percent of your pre-retirement income, each and every year of retirement. (This is called your income replacement rate.)

The exact percentage of income replacement depends on who you are and how much you earned before you retired. Lower-income people, for instance, will need a greater replacement rate (after all, food and medicine cost the same, no matter how much money you have), while higher-income workers need a little less to maintain their standard of living. But one fact is clear: less than half of workers are actually on track to achieve this essential replacement level of savings.[22]

The shortfalls are dramatic. As we mentioned earlier, people between the ages of 40 and 55 have an average retirement account balance of just $14,500[23]—a tiny fraction of the $400,000 the average worker needs for retirement.[24]

Those much nearer retirement age also fall far short. According to a recent study, 52 percent of households that include someone over 55 have no retirement savings.[25] The median balance held by retirees between 55 and 64 is only about $80,000.

Many retirees choose to convert their savings into an annuity—a financial instrument that essentially exchanges their savings for a guaranteed yearly income for the rest of their lives. However, if the median person retiring in their mid-60s converted their $80,000 in retirement savings to an annuity, it would require them to live on an income of only $2,000 per year—a paltry $166.67 a month.

It may be tempting to fault the savers for this dramatic gap, but it's wrong to "blame the victim." The fact is that most people simply cannot afford to save enough for retirement with the existing tools, and their employers don't contribute enough to fill the gap.

There are several reasons for this. One is that, for the last 40 years, median household income in America has been largely stagnant. In addition, the US has allowed its real minimum wage to plummet. In real terms, our minimum wage today is back where it was in the 1940s—a time when most workers were also eligible for a pension.

Visualizing the savings gap for Americans 40–55 years old.

$375,000

$14,500

Average Retirement
Savings

Retirement Savings
Needed

Sources: Center for American Progress (2015) "The Reality of the Retirement Crisis." Aon Hewitt (2012) "Retirement Income Adequacy at Large Companies: The Real Deal."

On top of these flat wages, the cost-based obstacles to saving for retirement are even greater now than they were in postwar America. For young savers and parents, education, child care, rent, and health-care costs are surging. Student loans are a much bigger burden than they were a half-century ago. The total outstanding student loan debt in this country today tops 1.3 trillion—a total that has nearly tripled in a decade. And for older savers, household debt is back on the rise after dipping in the wake of the Great Recession—recently reaching its highest levels since 2010.[26]

The burdens also land unevenly on men and women. Women tend to live longer than men, and so need greater savings for retirement. Yet at the same time, they face an even more challenging path to retirement security, because lower wages and interrupted careers make it difficult to save consistently.

The result is a greater likelihood of slipping into poverty in their old age. According to Diane Oakley, executive director of the Retirement Security Institute, "Women are 80 percent more likely than men to be impoverished at age 65 and older, while women between the ages of 75 and 79 are three times more likely than men to be living in poverty."[27]

In large part because of these headwinds, retirement savings rates continue to stagnate, even during the recent period of economic recovery.[28] Last year, for instance, a Federal Reserve survey asked Americans what they would do if faced with an emergency expense of just $400 tomorrow. Nearly half—47 percent—said they wouldn't be able to cover it unless they sold something or borrowed the money.[29]

2. People who do contribute to defined contribution plans are likely to draw savings before retirement—incurring high fees and taxes in the process.

The United States is one of the only nations that allows tax-preferred retirement savings—such as those you contribute to your 401(k)—to be withdrawn before retirement. In most countries, you can't withdraw your untaxed retirement funds early for any reason. In some countries, you can withdraw in the case of serious emergencies like life-altering illness. But in the US, you can withdraw your retirement savings practically whenever you want, for whatever reason—in exchange for a hefty tax penalty.

On its face, that might sound logical enough. It's your money, after all. But when American workers withdraw retirement savings early, there are high costs and taxes that significantly diminish savings.

There is a reason why this harmful access is not a feature of any sensible national retirement system in the rest of the world. For savers, it is just too tempting to make withdrawals before retirement, even though it seriously weakens their long-term financial security.

Indeed, a quick Google search of the term "withdraw 401k" reveals how ubiquitous this skimming phenomenon is.

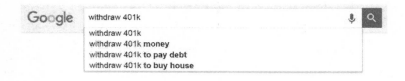

3. Under the current system, those participating in defined contribution plans experience subpar investment returns because of high fees and a structural bias toward short-term liquid stocks and bonds. Employees are forced to pay for liquidity they don't need, and they sacrifice larger returns in the process.

Because workers can withdraw retirement savings at any time, 401(k) administrators are required to offer only short-term instruments that offer a lot of liquidity, just in case a worker wants to withdraw his savings in a hurry. That structural bias toward short-term investments means retirement tools like 401(k)s and IRAs don't invest in

Historically, retirement savings strategies have delivered anemic returns compared to pension funds with more long-term strategies.

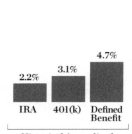

Historical Annualized
Rates of Return (2002–2012)

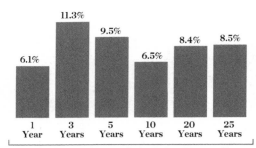

Median Public Pension Fund's Annualized Rates of Return
(as of 2014)

Source: Center for Retirement Research at Boston College (2015) "Investment Returns: Defined Benefit vs. Defined Contribution Plans." National Association of State Retirement Administrators (2015) "Issue Brief: Public Pension Plan Investment Return Assumptions."

Over time, endowments have also outperformed traditional short-term strategies, especially larger endowments with sizable allocations to alternatives.

	5 Years	10 Years	15 Years	20 Years	25 Years
Endowments over $1 Billion	3.8%	8.5%	8.1%	10.1%	10.4%
All Endowments	3.8%	6.8%	5.6%	7.7%	8.4%
All Active Balanced Mutual Funds	*5.1%*	*6%*	*4.9%*	*7%*	*7.9%*

Source: Vanguard Research (2014) "Assessing Endowment Performance: The Enduring Role of Low-Cost Investing."

The expected 5-year returns across traditional asset classes mean a typical stock and bond strategy will underperform compared to public pension funds.

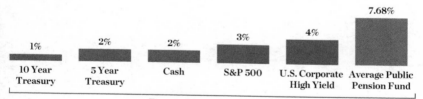

10 Year Treasury	5 Year Treasury	Cash	S&P 500	U.S. Corporate High Yield	Average Public Pension Fund
1%	2%	2%	3%	4%	7.68%

Expected Annualized Returns

Graph shows expected 5-year returns for key asset classes and assumed average rate of return for Public Pension Plans.

Source: Goldman Sachs (2016) "2015 Outlook: The Last Innings." Investment Management Division, Investment Strategy Group National Association of State Retirement Administrators (2015) Issue Brief: Public Pension Plan Investment Return Assumptions.

longer-term, less liquid alternatives such as hedge funds, private equity, and real estate. As a result, these plans deliver subpar returns compared to more alternative-focused strategies employed by pension funds and endowments.

The drawbacks of this system are clear. When you compare anticipated rates of return across a variety of asset classes, shorter-term options like Treasury bonds, high-yield corporate bonds, and a 60/40 stock and bond portfolio are all expected to deliver lower returns than longer-term public pension and university endowment investments.

Simply put, biasing investment portfolios toward high-liquidity investments is hurting workers by making it even more difficult to accumulate sufficient retirement savings.

4. The overall economy misses the full benefit of this capital because the short-termism favored by 401(k)s and IRAs inhibits long-term capital formation.

Excessive short-term investing is not just bad for America's retirees; it's bad for the entire nation. The accumulated retirement savings of the American people represent an enormous amount of capital that could be invested in everything from infrastructure to venture capital to real estate. These investments would greatly benefit our country—but our retirement system's structural bias toward short-term, high-liquidity investments makes this almost impossible.

We can see the consequences of this system by studying other nations. Countries that have enacted national retirement plans similar to our proposal report greater economic growth and stability. In Australia, national retirement savings actually exceed GDP, creating an economic ballast that helped the country avoid a market calamity in 2008. Susan Thorp, a professor at the University of Technology, Sydney, explains how:

> If you have people making regular contributions from their wages, there's always this steady stream of inflows into the capital markets . . . It's money that comes into the market to purchase securities regardless of conditions.[30]

There's no reason why the United States cannot adopt a similar approach. A recent survey found public sector pension funds in the United States—which, as we noted earlier, *do* invest for the long term—made up 20 percent of venture capital in 2014.[31] Defined contribution funds cannot play this same important role in our economy right now, but they should.

5. The current system features incentives that are upside down. The wealthy and financially sophisticated receive high tax subsidies; low-income and many middle-class workers receive none.

Every year, federal and state governments spend $140 billion to subsidize workers' pensions.[32] But these tax benefits do little to benefit workers most at risk. In fact, the only federal tax incentives that directly benefit savers are incredibly regressive.

These tax deductions reduce taxable income, directly and disproportionately benefitting the wealthiest Americans. The most affluent Americans get over 70 percent of the benefit from retirement tax deductions. Low-income workers who need the help get almost nothing.

It's not wealthier Americans who need the help. High net worth individuals benefit from better access to sophisticated, longer-term investment vehicles. These vehicles usually require a high minimum investment, so in practice, they are available only to those who can afford such a large investment.

Again, the incentives are entirely backward here. Our national retirement system should not be structured—intentionally or otherwise—to provide additional benefits for individuals who already enjoy a reliable path to a comfortable retirement.

6. Finally, even for financially sophisticated retirees, the current system offers no cost-effective means to convert retirement savings into lifelong income.

The current retirement system is simply not well set up for rising life expectancies. In 1950, the average woman lived for 15 years in retirement after reaching 65—the average man, 13. Today, women live for an average of 20 years in retirement, and men can expect to live for 17.[33]

This means that retirement savings have to last longer than ever—and that length of time continues to grow. Yet most people aren't able to plan for an uncertain life-span because they don't have the expertise to invest and annuitize their retirement savings properly. In fact, under the current system, retirees are disincentivized from pursuing annuities—financial instruments that guarantee an income disbursement every year in perpetuity—because of their high price tags.

The annuity plans currently available carry high costs because of the process of *adverse selection*. Like many complicated terms from economics, adverse selection describes a simple phenomenon: when you're selling something to a riskier customer, you can demand a higher price. Those with bad credit receive higher interest rates on a new mortgage. Older and sicker customers in the buyer pool face higher health insurance premiums. Similarly, in the current annuity marketplace, insurers anticipate that those who purchase annuities do so because they expect to live longer than average—and in anticipation of this longevity risk, insurers increase the cost of the annuity.[34]

Given these high costs—and the relatively complex process required to attain annuities—those who purchase annuities are generally more sophisticated investors. They tend to be more affluent individuals, rather than those most in need of retirement stability.[35]

In the following pages, we'll outline a solution that addresses all six of these problems and puts every American on the path to a sustainable retirement.

Rescuing Retirement

A Four-Pronged Solution

THE RETIREMENT SAVINGS PLAN AROSE FROM AN UNDER-
standing that America faces a generational choice, not unlike the
choice we faced before the enactment of Social Security—when the
prospect of millions of elderly Americans living in poverty loomed,
even before the Great Depression took its toll.

It was during this time that a young governor of New York, Franklin
Delano Roosevelt, declared:

> No greater tragedy exists in modern civilization than the aged,
> worn-out worker who, after a life of ceaseless effort and useful
> productivity, must look forward for his declining years to a poor-
> house. A modern social consciousness demands a more humane
> and efficient arrangement.[36]

Roosevelt was right then, and he still is. As a society, it's our
responsibility to answer his call once again. Indeed, in a world where

the specter of widespread elder poverty has returned, we have a stark choice. Either we will stick with the status quo and allow millions of our most hardworking citizens to end their lives in near or outright poverty, or we will seize the important opportunity that this moment represents to solve this problem relatively painlessly.

Who gets a GRA, and who contributes?

Under our plan, all those who don't have access to a workplace pension plan would be automatically enrolled into their own GRA. Those with 401(k)-type and all other plans would roll their savings over to a higher-performing GRA. This includes part-time and self-employed workers.

Since employee contributions are still crucial for guaranteeing a secure retirement, this system would require all businesses with over five employees to contribute either to a pension or GRA for each worker. Since the GRA features the smallest costs, we presume that most businesses will choose the GRA option. All firms that do not have a defined benefit plan will roll into a GRA within a five-year period.

However, the plan waives all employer contributions for businesses with fewer than five employees for five years—providing a safe haven for small business.

It all starts with individual savings. The foundation of the Retirement Savings Plan is something called a Guaranteed Retirement Account (GRA). These accounts are superior to 401(k)s, IRAs, and virtually all retirement instruments available today because they make contributions easier and significantly cheaper, and because they deliver a dramatically higher rate of return over time.

This new system represents a four-pronged solution to the retirement crisis.

1. The Retirement Savings Plan **ensures** that all workers can save enough to retire.

2. The Retirement Savings Plan **invests** those savings in lower-risk, longer-term strategies that generate a higher rate of return.

3. The Retirement Savings Plan **guarantees** lifelong annuitized benefits, no matter how long a retiree lives.

4. The Retirement Savings Plan would **reward** older Americans for working longer, if they are willing and able.

In the remainder of this section, we will look at these elements one at a time.

Retirement Fast Facts

Status Quo

$14,500	$375,000	16 Million	25 Million
Average retirement account balance of Americans age 40–55	Approximate amount the average American in typical circumstances needs to save to retire comfortably.	Retirees living in or near poverty by 2022	Retirees living in or near poverty by 2050

What Life Looks Like under the Retirement Savings Plan

$75	6–7%	Universal Coverage	$75,000
What it would cost the median-salary worker, after tax credits, for secure retirement	Expected annual, net-of-fees return for GRA savings—versus 2–4% return for 401(k)s and IRAs	Every worker will have their GRA as a workplace supplement to Social Security. This especially helps older women and others intermittently in the workforce.	Additional lifetime return on savings that a 25-year-old saving $600 a year could expect by age 65 under the Retirement Savings Plan.\n\nThat $600 per year would be completely offset by a tax credit, and thus costless, for almost all savers earning a median salary or less.

1. The Retirement Savings Plan ensures that all workers can save enough to retire.

Perhaps the most surprising fact about the current retirement crisis is that, despite widespread shortfalls, the additional yearly savings required for the average American to secure their retirement is relatively small. With a GRA system, Americans can be on the path to retirement easily.

Consider the math. Right now, workers save the equivalent of 12.5 percent of their annual income through Social Security. With the addition of a high-return GRA, we calculate that full-time workers need to save at least an additional 3 percent per year over the course of their careers to be able to maintain their standard of living in retirement.

This 3 percent number may seem smaller than you might assume. But it will be enough for most workers, because GRAs will invest these savings much more effectively than the current system. (We'll have more to say about this later.) The required incremental savings are much higher if they are invested through instruments like 401(k)s, for instance, because 401(k)s receive lower returns from investing in highly liquid securities. (Part-time workers will need to contribute a higher percentage of their income to have enough for retirement, as they do now.)

There is only one way to fill this 3 percent gap: the savings have to be mandated for all workers, including those who work part time and/or are self-employed.

A mandate may be a politically loaded approach these days, but workers are already comfortable with mandated retirement contributions—like Social Security! What's more, research and insights from the current retirement system make clear that nothing short of a mandate will provide future generations of Americans enough income for a secure retirement. And under our plan, for most Americans, this mandate is a gift—one that is both costless and priceless. Through the combination of a tax credit and tax deductions, the Retirement Savings Plan makes this contribution nearly free, for the government and for most individual Americans alike.

For most Americans, this mandate is a gift.

Meeting this 3 percent savings target begins by splitting the contribution between a 1.5 percent employee contribution and a 1.5 percent employer contribution—similar to how many employers contribute to worker 401(k) accounts today. Here's how this breakdown works.

What This 1.5 Percent Contribution Means for Employees

The employee's 1.5 percent contribution would be offset through two tax mechanisms, both of which would almost certainly be deficit- and revenue-neutral.

First, the RSP would create a new refundable $600 federal tax credit for all savers. This means that retirement security would be completely costless for a person earning $40,000 a year or less, because their annual contribution of 1.5 percent of income ($600) would be entirely offset by the credit.

For a worker earning America's median salary of $45,000 a year, 1.5 percent of income is $675. That leaves just $75 to contribute after the tax credit. This means the effective cost of retirement security would be just $75 per year to get $675 in your GRA—a nine-to-one multiple!

In addition to the $600 credit, the plan would allow any worker whose 1.5 percent contribution adds up to more than $600 to deduct the additional contribution from their taxes. For instance, a worker earning $80,000 per year would make a mandated contribution of $1,200. Of that contribution, $600 would be returned in a tax credit, and the remaining $600 would be tax deductible. That means they will be able to save $1,200, while paying only about $400—a 3:1 ratio of savings to cost.

How are these tax benefits revenue-neutral?

The federal government already spends $120 billion each year on tax deductions for defined contribution plans (while states spend $20 billion)—but these federal deductions disproportionately benefit the wealthiest Americans. The Retirement Savings Plan simply redirects much of this existing tax spending, offering meaningful retirement savings support to those who need it most.

In addition, tackling the retirement crisis head-on will create savings for taxpayers in the long run. By reducing the number of seniors burdening programs like Medicaid, public housing, and the Supplemental Nutrition Assistance Program (SNAP), for instance, the GRA system would significantly reduce federal spending in the future. (For more on the RSP's revenue neutrality, see appendix A.)

The GRA system is structured to work well for savers across the income spectrum. For high-income workers, the *obligation* to contribute to the GRA would be capped at $3,750—which is 1.5 percent of an annual salary cap of $250,000 of income. They would still get their $600 tax credit and be able to deduct the remaining $3,150, almost a 2:1 ratio of savings to cost.

However, all workers would be free to make additional GRA contributions beyond the required amount, and we anticipate that many would and most should. There is no maximum limit on annual contributions, and individuals may find it convenient and profitable to save as much as possible in their professionally managed, low-fee GRA. It's important to note, however, that the tax deferrals are limited to the mandatory contribution amounts.

For all savers, the employee contribution would be automatically deducted from their payroll, similar to current retirement plans.

What This 1.5 Percent Contribution Means for Employers

Employers will find the GRA model to be a great asset to their business. Employers today fear that offering retirement plans will put them at a competitive disadvantage. And many employers face the same complexity as individuals; often the hassle of navigating brokers and plans inhibits their ability to effectively provide for their employees. This is especially true for small-business owners.

The GRA model simplifies the process significantly. As noted earlier, the plan requires employers to contribute 1.5 percent by providing either a traditional pension plan or a GRA. The GRA features the smallest costs for the most effective returns, so we presume that most businesses will choose this option. All firms that do not have a defined benefit plan will be automatically rolled into a GRA after five years.

This employer contribution will be affordable—or even costless—for a number of reasons:

- Employers would deduct their share of the GRA contributions, similar to how they deduct pension and other retirement expenses today.

- The cost of the employer contribution would be substantially offset by ending burdensome workplace administration of existing retirement plans. For many employers, there will be no increase in costs, because they will be relieved of having to manage and contribute to their own 401(k) plans—often at significantly higher rates than 1.5 percent.

- For employers who have no provision for their employees' retirement, there would be a modest increase in costs that could be covered with a price increase of just 1–2 percent. With inflation widely regarded as too low and corporate profits as a percentage of GDP at an all-time high, this retirement contribution for employers should be readily affordable.

- The employer would also be required to make its contribution only to the first $250,000 of an employee's wages—though it would be free to contribute more.

- Finally, the GRA model forestalls the need for much higher corporate taxes in the future to deal with the retirement crisis that would otherwise overwhelm government finances. In that way, the plan is a smart trade-off for businesses.

The Retirement Savings Plan also includes provisions that benefit low-wage workers and small businesses:

- For low-wage hourly workers, the plan sets the employer contribution at a minimum of 20 cents per hour.

- For businesses with fewer than five employees, the employer contribution would be waived for the first five years of the plan.

For those who are self-employed, in partnerships, or for Subchapter S corporations, the individual is responsible for both the employer and employee contribution, just as in Social Security. This is because in most cases, these workers are individuals who average high earnings or for whom earnings are supplemental income. And because this plan is universal, employers don't need to worry about being placed at a disadvantage to their competitors.

Imagine, for instance, what would happen if Social Security was not mandated: all employers who paid FICA would be disadvantaged by competing with employers who did not. This unfair competition is the cause of the market disruption rocking the voluntary pension system today. The Retirement Savings Plan removes the competitive disadvantage from doing the right thing—and therefore lifts barriers for many employers.

Let's pause to answer a quick question. Does the GRA provide sufficient incentives to savers?

Yes, absolutely, especially when you compare it to today's system. Under the current retirement patchwork, the government is disproportionately subsidizing the retirement savings of the wealthiest Americans. Under the Retirement Savings Plan, all savers have the chance to deduct their 1.5 percent contributions—if they're not already offset completely by the tax credit.

Many may decide that they want to put aside more than the 3 percent contribution rate to maintain their desired lifestyle. One of the key strengths of the plan is that, on top of the 1.5 percent mandate, all savers would also be encouraged to contribute additional funds to their GRA each year, if they would like to and are able.

Employers would also be able to voluntarily contribute more if they desire. It's likely that many employers would increase their contribution in order to attract and retain quality employees—similar to how many employers currently offer 401(k) contributions upwards of 3 or 4 percent.

What's more, evidence from similar retirement systems around the globe—Australia, in particular—suggests that systems do not have to match or tax-incent every dollar in order for people to save. Since many people will want to contribute more than 3 percent to their retirement plan, the GRA is a safe, convenient, and high-performing option already at their fingertips.

Indeed, after people have established a rainy-day fund that they can access anytime—usually in a standard savings account or a myRA—a GRA would be one of the best places to save additional income that they want to put away for the future. Unlike depositing that extra income into a savings account, putting it into a GRA would mean it has the benefit of a higher return.

2. The Retirement Savings Plan invests those savings in lower-risk, longer-term strategies that generate a higher rate of return.

Once workers accumulate savings, their money can—and must—work harder for them. 401(k) and IRA plans simply don't perform well enough; the fees are too high and typical portfolios are not diversified. The Retirement Savings Plan corrects this problem in the current system, equipping savers to earn meaningfully higher rates of return on their GRAs, without increased risk.

People's money can—and must —work harder for them.

Without compromising each person's direct ownership of their GRA savings, our plan would invest that money as part of a broader strategic investment pool, combining retirement savings from other GRAs across the country. This is effective because, when people combine their funds, they also increase their investing power. With a larger pool of assets, investors are able to build more diversified portfolios, access institutional-quality investment products, and leverage economies of scale in order to reduce management fees. The result is better returns than those individuals could achieve on their own.

The GRA mobilizes the power of competition. Under the GRA model, individuals would also be able to choose their own manager from a national exchange. Managers could include private-sector money management firms, state agencies that manage public pensions, or possibly a self-funded federal entity.

Individual holders would select their GRA pension manager based on fees and investment performance. They would be able to choose their preferred manager or change from one to another once a year. Accounts would be fully portable, and the assets would transfer, based on the account balance. A national exchange of managers, administered by an existing federal agency, would be the best way to facilitate this process.

Managing the Guaranteed Retirement Accounts in a pooled fashion is beneficial for savers for three reasons.

First, pooled investments leverage economies of scale to pay lower fees. Indeed, as a recent study found, "[f]or some plans, the annual savings from transitioning from retail to institutional shares may be as high as 65 basis points per year."[37]

Second, the larger pool of capital would also offer greater access to high-quality portfolio managers who will compete to generate the best return. When plan participants have access to professional asset managers, their portfolios earn a median annual return 3.32 percent higher than those that do not.[38]

Third, and perhaps most important, these investment strategists would be able to adopt long-term investment horizons that generate the best results. The GRA pool could be invested in opportunities typically reserved for institutional investors—less liquid, higher-return asset classes. These include high-yielding and risk-reducing alternative asset classes.

Moving toward these types of investment products not only enhances returns but provides significant downside protection in bad markets—reducing overall portfolio risk. In other words, they can both increase return and decrease risk.

When institutions making use of this longer-term investment strategy are surveyed, the superior returns are clear:

- A brief by the National Association of State Retirement Administrators found that public pension funds delivered an 8.5 percent median rate of return over a 25-year investment period.

- A Vanguard survey of university endowments—which have a similar long-term investment horizon—found similar success: an average return of 8.4 percent over a 25-year period.

It's important to enable this kind of strategy, because individuals need to pool their risks. A well-designed retirement savings vehicle managed by professionals will allow savers to take prudent amounts of risk—particularly when it comes to long-term investments. That's why this plan facilitates risk sharing and risk exposure over long-term cycles in pooled plans managed by professionals.

Because savers would make similar-sized contributions that would be invested every year, GRAs would have the benefit of the long-term dollar-cost averaging investment strategy. With the same amount of capital put to work each year, investors automatically buy more in weak markets (prices are lower) and less in peak markets (when prices are high). This pattern of investing runs counter to most people's natural tendency, but it is important because it dampens swings in investment returns over time.

Alternatives reduce risk for a given level of return.

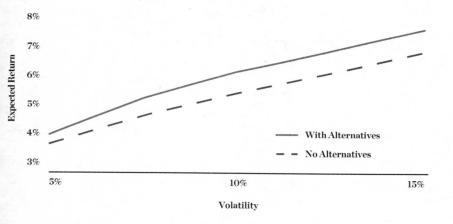

Source: Aon Hewitt Investment Consulting (2013) "Alternative Assets: The Next Frontier for Defined Contribution Plans." Idea Development Forum.

A survey of the largest public pension funds shows a substantial majority assume future investment returns between 7% and 8%.

Graph shows the distribution of investment return assumptions from NASRA's Public Fund Survey, 2015.

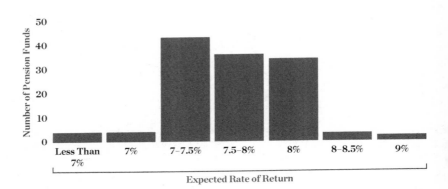

Source: National Association of State Retirement Administrators (2015) "Issue Brief: Public Pension Plan Investment Return Assumptions."

As mentioned above, the structure of today's 401(k) plans and IRAs makes this kind of strategic investing impossible. These types of defined contribution plans are required to be invested in ways that force excess liquidity, with short-term investment horizons, lots of volatility, and high administrative costs.

The difference between a well-managed long-term strategy and a short-term suboptimal one is dramatic. Existing defined contribution plans tend to earn, after fees, only 2–3 percent annually. But by investing with a longer-term approach, we believe the GRAs can target a rate of return of 6–7 percent.

Of course, it is impossible to know with absolute certainty exactly what the pooled assets will earn. But decades of past performance suggest that a pooled long-term fund will significantly outperform today's defined contribution returns.

The beauty of investing more effectively is that higher returns would go a long way toward closing the retirement gap without taking any extra money out of a saver's paycheck, meaningfully increasing the employer's costs, or adding to the government deficit. For a 25-year-old worker saving $1,000 per year, for instance, a shift in investment strategy that raised the return from 3 percent to 6.5 percent would mean the difference between $75,000 and $200,000 in savings by the time he or she reaches age 65. Over long periods of time, even seemingly modest differences in rates of return have a powerful effect on the ultimate amount of retirement savings.

Modest differences in rate of return can create significantly different savings over time.

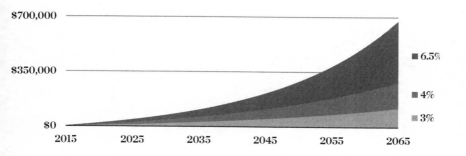

Source: Based on authors' calculations.

With the understanding that many savers are still fearful for their nest egg, the Retirement Savings Plan takes an extra step to make GRA savings one of the safest savings options available. Under the GRA system, at the time of retirement, the federal government would guarantee that each saver's principal is protected and, at a minimum, that they get back as much as they put in upon retirement.

This guarantee would do two things. First, it would smooth the threat of market volatility if someone retires at a bad time in the markets. Second, it would engender confidence in the system.

The principal protection guarantee does not protect the GRA from losses in any single year or even in multiple years. It simply means that, over the forty- to fifty-year life-span of the account, workers would be entitled to a minimum compounded return of their principal contributions over that period.

This guarantee would function as a onetime test at the time of retirement, when the GRA is being annuitized. The guarantee is not discretionary or optional; it will simply go into the calculation of the annuity by increasing payments if the GRA has failed to meet the principal amounts contributed. Only the mandatory payment to the GRAs will be covered by this guarantee. This includes the money that will be deposited when employees roll their 401(k) savings into GRAs.

While this sounds like a big commitment by the government, it's a promise that will be essentially costless, because the accounts are highly likely to perform significantly better than 0 percent over the long term. We analyzed every rolling 40 year period since 1945, and there was not a single one in which the guarantee would have been triggered—even for seniors who retired in the midst of the global financial crisis.

All the same, the government could charge a small insurance premium to cover these unlikely costs, if desired. A fee of 0.015 percent of pay—less than $10 a year for a worker making $65,000—would build a reserve fund that would cover virtually all potential costs in even the most extreme scenarios. (For more details on why the guarantee is essentially costless, see appendix B.)

3. The Retirement Savings Plan guarantees lifelong annuitized benefits, no matter how long a retiree lives.

A well designed retirement plan is built for lifetime income. Unfortunately, even among those who manage to save and invest their savings effectively, most people do not have the expertise to annuitize their savings when they retire. The Retirement Savings Plan solves this problem, helping savers make the right choices to secure guaranteed income for the rest of their lives.

Under the current 401(k) model, the retiree shoulders all the burden of post-retirement asset management:

- The individual must determine how best to invest and annuitize his or her retirement savings, which is a complex decision that most people cannot be expected to make.

- The individual must bear the risk that the insurance company paying the annuity may not remain solvent decades into the future.

- The individual must shoulder the higher administrative costs of today's ineffective annuity marketplace.

The Retirement Savings Plan addresses these burdens by automatically annuitizing individuals' accumulated savings when they retire or become disabled. Individuals would then receive a guaranteed amount based on their savings for as long as they live.

The GRA model's pooled ecosystem makes these annuities possible, because participants don't just pool their savings—they also pool their risk of running out of money in old age. In a nationwide retirement pool, actuarial risks are shared and mitigated, costs are spread, and everyone benefits by essentially insuring against outliving retirement savings.

For beneficiaries under a GRA, the transition to retirement will look and feel much like the experience under a defined benefit pension plan. Retirees will have confidence that, while the amount may change, their benefit check will never fall below a set minimum amount.

The GRA model provides both greater expected returns and more secure financial stability throughout retirement.

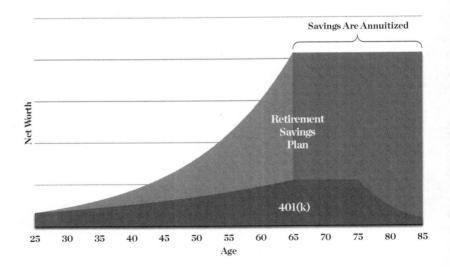

This restores what workers liked best about the defined benefit system—certainty and peace of mind in retirement—and shifts the burden of post-retirement planning away from the individual. This alone has tangible benefits. Economic and medical research shows that older people experience a greater degree of well-being when their income is assured and steady rather than when they are left to manage lumps of cash with variable returns.

Guaranteed income, no matter how long a retiree or his/her spouse lives.

Annuitization also means an end to the challenge posed by rising life expectancies. Today, retirees have to stretch their savings 15–20 years, on average, but under the current defined contribution model, retirees are on their own if savings run out.

Individuals are in control of when to annuitize their GRA. Options include the age of disability, at 62—Social Security's early retirement age—or at any age up until age 70, when Social Security benefits are at their maximum. Individuals can annuitize their GRA without collecting Social Security—making it affordable for more Americans to wait to collect Social Security in exchange for a higher benefit.

Far from requiring a new bureaucracy, the annuities themselves—though individually owned—would be purchased from the US government, and the payments themselves would be physically made by existing Social Security Administration infrastructure. This system can be implemented without adding to the federal bureaucracy or creating a new government agency. In fact, with more assets under administration, costs per person should actually decrease.

Fast Facts about the GRA Annuity

Annuitization won't keep you from going back to work.
If a retiree returns to work, he or she would start a new GRA, while continuing to receive his/her old annuity payments. Upon retiring a second time, the value of the second GRA would be added to the existing annuity.

Each worker's annuity would take into account his or her age and family structure at the date of retirement.
For instance, if a single, older retiree and a younger couple had the same GRA balance, the single older person would get larger annual payments. This approach means every worker gets the full value of their GRA, taking into account their particular circumstances.

Annuity payments would be calculated in a way that minimizes the risk of annuity rates being particularly low at the time the worker retires.
When calculating federal annuity payments for each retiree, the plan will use the trailing five-year average long-term Treasury bond rate as the discount rate. This will smooth out the volatility in annuity rates that people would otherwise face at retirement.

Annuities enhance
retiree satisfaction.[39]

Not having a lifelong pension to supplement Social Security takes its toll on Americans through increased anxiety. This fear of outliving one's retirement savings even reaches those who have defined contribution plans. Unlike annuities, which guarantee a stream of income for life, DC plans burden retirees with the task of ensuring that their lump sum of retirement savings doesn't run out before the end of their lives. Not surprisingly, this causes those with DC plans to report lower levels of well-being.

Let's compare two 65-year-olds who are alike in every way except in the form of their $250,000 retirement plan. One retiree has a $250,000 IRA that he has to manage to last the rest of his life. The other has a pension valued at $250,000 that pays $1,500 per month for the rest of his life no matter how long he lives. Who is happier? Hands down, the research shows it is the retiree with the lifelong guaranteed annuity. Economists Steve Nyce and Billie Jean Quade find in "Annuities and Retirement Happiness" that when comparing retirees with similar levels of health and wealth, those with annuitized incomes are the happiest.

Annuities help retirees with less wealth and those in poor health feel more satisfied with their lives. Nyce and Quade updated, expanded, and confirmed earlier findings from Rand and Boston College[40] that secure lifetime benefits caused less anxiety among older people than lump sums. Economists Constantijn Panis from the Rand Institute and Kevin Bender and Natalia Jivan from the Center for Retirement Research in 2000 and 2005 find that retirees who are most satisfied tend to be older, have traditional pension annuities, and had the flexibility to choose when to retire. In 2003, Panis found annuities provide more satisfaction than equivalently valued lump sums.[41] Bender and Jivan conclude that while income and wealth increase overall well-being, the effect is relatively small compared to having guaranteed income for life. Having a defined benefit plan that provides a lifetime annuity has a positive impact on the well-being of retirees, compared to having no pension or just a defined contribution plan.[42]

The Employee Benefit Research Institute's ongoing survey about retirement confidence consistently shows that having a retirement plan is the most important factor in whether older workers are confident they will have enough money and security in retirement. Bloomberg News journalist Christopher Flavelle reports on a survey from Bankrate that suggests retirement anxiety is the new "class divide." People who earn more than $75,000 per year are three times more confident that they are saving enough compared to the bottom 80 percent.[43]

4. The Retirement Savings Plan would reward older Americans for working longer, if they are willing and able.

No one should ever be forced to leave the workforce before they're ready. That's why, through a combination of employer incentives and employee savings bonuses, the Retirement Savings Plan empowers older workers to stay in the workforce if they want to. That way, savers have more time to save for retirement, are able to make larger contributions, and face fewer years in retirement over which to stretch their non-GRA savings.

No one should be forced to leave the workforce before they're ready.

Retiring later would remain entirely optional. We are in no way suggesting raising the Social Security age, and we also recognize that working longer is not a viable option for everyone. People with medical issues or those working dangerous or physically demanding jobs, for instance, may not be able to work later in life. But for many, working longer has financial, emotional, and health benefits. The Retirement Savings Plan would facilitate this option for many more people.

On the employee end, our plan would provide that all GRA contributions made in years worked past the age of 65 would enjoy a doubled credit—every dollar counts twice! This incentive would stay in effect as long as a worker remains in the workforce, up to age 70. This has the benefit of providing older workers with a reason to delay collection of Social Security and GRA payments and also provides a significant boost to their overall retirement savings.

On the employer end, the Retirement Savings Plan would make Medicare the primary health coverage for workers over 65, even if they keep working. This way, employers who pay health insurance will get a large break on their insurance cost for every employee past Medicare age. Instead of paying about $25,000 for an older worker's health insurance costs, the employer would pay $2,000 to $5,000 for a Medicare supplement. That is a significant incentive for employers to try to keep older employees on the payroll longer. This is a simple change that comes without significant cost to the government—after all, Medicare would have been paying anyway, had the worker retired.

Two Paths to Retirement for an American Worker

Current Model

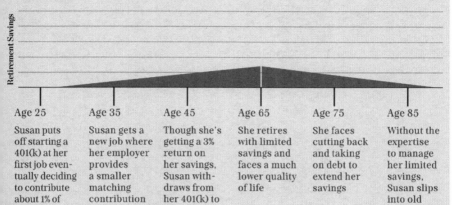

Retirement Savings

Age 25	Age 35	Age 45	Age 65	Age 75	Age 85
Susan puts off starting a 401(k) at her first job eventually deciding to contribute about 1% of her salary every year	Susan gets a new job where her employer provides a smaller matching contribution	Though she's getting a 3% return on her savings, Susan withdraws from her 401(k) to purchase a new car	She retires with limited savings and faces a much lower quality of life	She faces cutting back and taking on debt to extend her savings	Without the expertise to manage her limited savings, Susan slips into old age poverty

GRA Savings Model

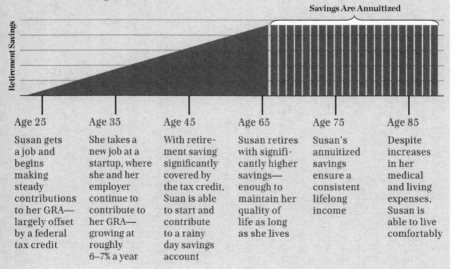

Retirement Savings

Savings Are Annuitized

Age 25	Age 35	Age 45	Age 65	Age 75	Age 85
Susan gets a job and begins making steady contributions to her GRA—largely offset by a federal tax credit	She takes a new job at a startup, where she and her employer continue to contribute to her GRA—growing at roughly 6–7% a year	With retirement saving significantly covered by the tax credit, Suan is able to start and contribute to a rainy day savings account	Susan retires with significantly higher savings—enough to maintain her quality of life as long as she lives	Susan's annuitized savings ensure a consistent lifelong income	Despite increases in her medical and living expenses, Susan is able to live comfortably

What about Social Security?

Social Security is the foundation on which this plan is built; they work together to guarantee retirement security for all Americans.

We believe it's essential that Congress take action to shore up Social Security's finances for generations to come. However, this is only one step we need to ensure retirement security across our country.

Yes, Social Security works!

But even a fully funded Social Security program on its own it is not enough.

Social Security is the basis of retirement security for most Americans. It has many strengths.

But Social Security was designed as a redistributive safety net for those facing poverty in old age. The middle class, in contrast, was supposed to rely on prefunded pensions as the primary pillar of retirement. That is the pillar we must restore today.

Why not just "fix" Social Security?

There are several reasons why setting up a GRA system to act in concert with Social Security is a better option for America's future retirees than simply expanding the Social Security program on its own.

First, expanding Social Security would require raising taxes or increasing the deficit. The GRA model, on the other hand, is budget-neutral, empowering employees to place their own money in their own account. For those earning less than the median wage, their contribution would be almost completely offset by a tax credit. For employers, their contribution would be offset by the savings from no longer administering retirement plans.

Second, unlike Social Security, GRAs rely on actual cash in every person's individually owned retirement savings account. Real capital means real, high-performing investments that can close the retirement savings gap without adding to the deficit.

Third, expanding Social Security would likely lift up just the poorest elderly Americans. But retirement security is a problem for people of virtually all income levels. GRAs are add-on accounts that provide the tools for a secure and comfortable retirement for everyone across the income spectrum.

Finally, there is no political consensus on either the goals or the fixes for Social Security. GRAs work within the existing system to guarantee retirement security.

Case Studies
Similar Plans in Action

WE KNOW A RETIREMENT SYSTEM LIKE THE RETIREMENT Savings Plan can work, because we've seen models just like it work all over the world. Some are even working right now, in limited ways, in certain states across America.

An Australian Case Study

Retirement observers see Australia's Superannuation Guarantee[44]—a mandated retirement savings system with many similarities to our proposed Guaranteed Retirement Accounts—as a potential road map for America.[45] And with good reason: it has worked incredibly well.

As recently as the 1980s, Australia's retirement system was similar to where the United States' is today, with less than half the workforce covered by pension plans.[46] Many more Australians were falling short in retirement, just as millions of American seniors are falling short today.[47]

In response to that reality and an aging population, Australia pursued a solution that was relatively novel at that point: the nation began to mandate retirement savings.

In 1992, Australia implemented its mandatory, national super-annuation savings program. Under this model, employers now automatically contribute 9.5 percent of a worker's salary to a long-term retirement savings account. That percentage is set to rise to 10 percent in 2021 and 12 percent in 2025. Workers are encouraged to contribute even more if they can.[48]

A little more than two decades in, the success of the Australian model is clear. Before this system was enacted, less than half of Australian workers—and only 23 percent of low-income workers like construction workers and clerks—had retirement pensions. Today, all Australian workers are covered by a retirement plan. The program now has nearly AU$2 trillion in savings—almost as much as Australia's total gross domestic product.[49]

User satisfaction is high and on the rise. In 2015, 59 percent of Australians said they were either very or fairly satisfied with the performance of their retirement savings—up from 53.3 percent in 2013.[50]

It's not a perfect system, of course, and there are lessons to be learned there, too. Upon retirement, Australian savers have the option to structure their benefit as either a lump sum, a phased withdrawal, or an annuity. One expert has noted that the "lack of annuitization makes older Australians heavily exposed to longevity, inflation, and investment risks."[51] This underlines how important it is for a retirement system to ensure a consistent lifetime income as well as lifelong savings—as the Retirement Savings Plan would in the United States.

Even with this weakness, however, the Australian model far out-strips most of the world. Australia's retirement system now trails only Denmark and the Netherlands on key measures of effectiveness, sustainability, and integrity.[52] By contrast, the American system lags far behind, joining countries like Mexico and South Africa in a tier designated for retirement systems with "some good features" but also with "major risks and/or shortcomings that should be addressed."[53]

Retirement Plans in the United States

With federal action lacking, over 26 states (as of late spring 2016) in the United States have taken action to address the retirement crisis, with a few moving toward a GRA-style model. States like Washington and Illinois have enacted plans that mandate (with an opt-out provision) retirement savings.

For its part, the Obama administration has worked to encourage this approach by clearing regulatory hurdles. "We want to do everything we can to encourage more states to take this step," President Obama said just last year. "We've got to make it easier for people to save for retirement."[54]

These state-based experiments are already poised for some promising success. "We know these plans work, because people are 15 times more likely to save by having access to payroll deduction," an AARP expert noted to the *New York Times*.[55]

But it's important to remember that states are being forced to act in the absence of federal legislation—and state systems do not benefit from the same economies of scale as a national model.[56] These state efforts are important experiments, and their champions should be celebrated, but it must also be recognized that coordinated regulation, management, asset pooling, and risk management of these retirement accounts would all be cheaper and more effective on a national scale.

States remain the laboratory of democracy, but the scale and immediacy of the retirement crisis demand a nationwide solution. It will require federal legislation—and national leadership—to bring that change about.

Growing Support from the American People and a Mandate For Congress

WE'RE EXCITED ABOUT THIS PLAN, AND WE'VE PUT A LOT of thought into it. We've considered all of the eventualities that would need to be addressed, the protections and guarantees that would have to be put into place, and the costs that would need to be accounted for. We hope you're as excited about this plan as we are, but you might also be thinking, "That's great as an intellectual exercise, but do you really expect Congress, which seems not to act on anything, to act on something like this? And isn't the retirement issue too politically charged to expect any action?"

It's easy to get dispirited by the scope of the retirement challenge America faces, but we believe that this plan is politically viable for a number of reasons.

First, this plan doesn't touch any third rails. It does not attempt to alter Social Security, nor does it attempt to address other serious issues we face, such as underemployment, wealth disparity, or stagnant middle-class incomes. However, it does provide an actionable solution to one of the most daunting threats to our economic future. It will relieve our welfare programs from undue strain and free up revenue for other pressing needs.

Second, America's retirement crisis will become a huge political issue—with consequences for elected officials—if not addressed. Retirement worries pervade all segments of American society, including among many people with seemingly high incomes. If implemented, this solution will have resounding impact on more than half of all working Americans, including those most at risk of retirement insolvency. Not many other significant policy reform proposals can say the same thing.

Third, and perhaps most important, the American people are calling for a national retirement solution.

According to a 2015 survey, 86 percent of Americans "believe that the nation faces a retirement crisis," 84 percent want "national policymakers to give more attention to retirement issues," and 67 percent say that they "would be willing to take less in salary increases in exchange for guaranteed income in retirement."[57] It's not just one poll, either. These survey results are echoed by Gallup, which finds that retirement is America's top financial worry. In 2014, 59 percent said they were very or moderately worried about having enough money to retire.

Gallup also found big changes in workers' retirement expectations. Thirty-seven percent expect to work past the age of 65, up from 14 percent in 1996.[58] Another poll found 36 percent believe Social Security will be a "major source of retirement income," up 10 percent from 2005.[59]

These are not numbers that favor the status quo—nor are they numbers that suggest Americans are unrealistic or nostalgic in their approach to retirement. The American people understand change is necessary, and they are prepared to embrace it.

Congressman Joe Crowley, a Democrat from New York, has introduced legislation that would greatly expand federal retirement savings options.[60] Legislation like this—with a few key adaptations like those discussed in our plan—would form a foundation for a comprehensive federal retirement solution. It would be a plan built on the best ideas of both parties: a policy proposal with clear bipartisan appeal.

The time has come for action. The retirement crisis is looming—and the public appetite for strong federal action to tackle it is apparent.

The Retirement Savings Plan can have bipartisan appeal.

- Helps working Americans

- Addresses a massive issue that cuts across all demographics

- Not an entitlement

- Not a new bureaucracy

- Won't increase the deficit

- GRAs are individual accounts with personal ownership and oversight.

- They are virtually costless for most individuals.

- The plan offers additional benefits of widespread capital formation.

- Supports small businesses

- Politicians on both sides of the aisle have supported broadly similar policies.

Conclusion

AMERICA'S RETIREMENT CRISIS MAY BE DAUNTING, BUT IT is by no measure insurmountable. We have all of the tools we need to solve this problem—we just need to put them into action.

At this moment, in fact, we already have access to a solution that is remarkably simple, immediately effective, and already has considerable bipartisan support. By enacting a national system of Guaranteed Retirement Accounts, we can guarantee most Americans a comfortable retirement. We can help workers save enough to retire—delivering a higher rate of return and annuitizing benefits to protect retirees no matter how long they live. And we can do all this in a way that costs the government next to nothing and requires virtually no new bureaucracy.

All that is missing—at least for now—is political will to solve this crisis while we still can.

Will we act now, while there is still time? Or will we wait for the chilling statistics to become tragic human stories?

If we act now, we have time to build up savings gradually and the cost will be modest. If we wait, there will be a crisis down the road and the cost will be huge.

It is rare that a program can simultaneously be sweeping and deficit-neutral, visionary and practical. But that's what we've designed in this book.

The Retirement Savings Plan offers a chance for millions of Americans to have a stronger, more stable retirement—and a chance to set this country on a sustainable retirement trajectory for generations to come.

Questions and Answers about the Retirement Savings Plan

Does this plan work for those approaching retirement age currently or within the next decade?

Because it relies on a lifetime of higher investment returns, this plan will be most effective for those who have several decades to save for retirement. However, everyone would benefit from saving more and earning higher returns in advance of retirement, no matter their age.

Even people in their fifties who start saving now can use those savings in retirement to delay collecting Social Security benefits and to supplement the benefits they do get. And when you delay collecting Social Security benefits between the ages of 62 and 70, you get a guaranteed increase in benefits when you do start collecting them. (The longer you wait to begin collecting Social Security benefits, the higher the reward. For example, if an individual has $20,000 available and delays collecting Social Security until age 65, he or she will experience a lifetime increase in earnings of over 12 percent.)

The plan also gives workers approaching retirement an enticing reason to stay in the workforce a little longer than they otherwise would have. The benefits they stand to gain from up to an additional seven years of work under the Retirement Savings Plan allows for a much more comfortable retirement.

Are low-wage workers treated fairly under this plan?

The plan is significantly fairer to low-wage workers than the status quo and would guarantee that greater retirement savings would be functionally costless for almost every household below the median American salary. (See appendix A.)

The Plan directly supports low-wage workers in two ways. First, the refundable tax credit offsets a worker's contribution into the GRA up to $600 every year—significantly fairer than the current tax deduction model. Second, for low-wage earners, the plan sets the employer contribution (normally 1.5 percent) at a minimum of 20 cents per hour, further augmenting their retirement savings.

Will people be vulnerable if the market has a downturn?

Under the Retirement Savings Plan, the government will guarantee that each person retiring has saved at least their mandated principal contributions at retirement. This way, even if someone retires during a serious market downturn, his or her retirement savings will be protected. However, it is overwhelmingly likely that GRAs will earn much more—around 6–7 percent—so in practice, this guarantee should be virtually costless. (See appendix B.)

Could the 3 percent savings mandate be raised in the future?

Evidence suggests that people saving 3 percent of their income, invested and earning a decent return over time, will have sufficient savings to continue their quality of life in retirement. However, if circumstances in the future indicate that greater baseline savings are necessary, policymakers will have the option to recalibrate the savings mandate. In other countries, contribution rates have been raised over time because the plans have been so popular.

Do savers legally own their GRAs?

Yes. It is important for savers to know the money in their GRA is truly theirs, and that ownership should be legally explicit. GRAs will be prevented from being garnished by a creditor as loan collateral.

Can a spouse inherit a deceased partner's GRA?

Regardless of whether an individual passes away before or after their GRA annuitization, our plan ensures that the surviving spouse is cared for. In the event of a death that occurs before annuitization, the surviving spouse simply inherits the GRA in full. The annuitization process occurs on the household level, factoring in family size and longevity assumptions. Therefore, deaths that occur after annuitization would not alter the surviving spouse's GRA benefit—ensuring one less worry during a tragic and painful time.

Can a non-retiree withdraw from a GRA in the case of an emergency?

To function well, the GRA model must work similarly to a defined benefit pension plan and prevent pre-retirement withdrawals. However, the myRA provides an option for people seeking to establish a rainy day fund—and that option will continue under the plan.

Is it fair to encourage people to work longer?

Participation in the labor force over the age of 65 would remain purely voluntary. This plan does nothing other than give older workers who might wish to work longer a benefit for doing so.

What is truly unfair is giving Americans no effective means to save for retirement, then expecting them to find a way to get by for decades once they stop working. That's what the current system offers. The

Retirement Savings Plan is built on a recognition of a new retirement reality. At a time when people are living longer than ever, their retirement savings have to last longer, too. Delaying retirement makes this feasible by giving workers more time to accumulate savings, make larger contributions, have more time for those savings to earn returns and grow, and face fewer years in retirement over which to stretch their retirement savings. It also means that their ultimate benefit from Social Security will be greater.

Who would be responsible for investing the funds? Is this plan a way to get more money for Wall Street to manage?

Individual savers will choose their own manager, and there will be many to choose from—including traditional money management firms, mutual fund companies, state agencies that now manage public pension plans, a self-funded, national entity that could potentially be set up by the federal government, and maybe even Berkshire Hathaway!—all competing for your business.

This new class of "pension managers" would work like endowment and pension plan administrators. They would focus on asset allocation, risk management, and the selection of individual investment managers and subadvisors to handle the actual buying and selling of particular investments. These managers would have a fiduciary obligation to the GRA holders and would need to be federally licensed and regulated.

Individual GRA holders would select their pension manager based on fees and investment performance. They would be able to choose their preferred manager or change from one to another once per year. Accounts would be fully portable and the assets would transfer based on the account balance. A national exchange of managers would be the best way to facilitate this process.

A cottage industry could even arise to advise GRA holders and rate different managers (similar to Morningstar and mutual funds).

Some states have enacted their own retirement plans. Isn't that enough?

While these efforts are admirable, there are several reasons why a true solution must be a national one. Retirement savings must be portable and consistent across state lines. The Retirement Savings Plan is tied to federal taxation by redeploying federal tax deductions into federal tax credits and uses the Social Security infrastructure for its administration.

In addition, the economies of scale of a nationwide plan make the entire system cheaper to administer and likely to generate a significantly higher return for savers.

Does the combination of mandating GRAs and ending tax breaks for 401(k)s and IRAs take retirement savings decisions out of the hands of individuals?

No. Each individual will control his or her own account. For too long, the American people have been left on their own when it comes to preparing for retirement. That's why almost no one is prepared for retirement today. The word "mandate" may be politically charged these days, but research and experience make it clear that it's the only thing that will work.

Is it more practical to simply expand Social Security or existing federal options like myRA?

Social Security does provide workers with a base level of security, and we don't propose changing that. That's why the Retirement Savings Plan would be an addition to, not a replacement for, Social Security.

However, Social Security was designed as a safety net for those facing poverty in old age. It was never meant to be a vehicle to guarantee a middle-class retirement—and it's not the best one to do so. There are four key reasons why.

First, expanding Social Security may help to take care of the very poorest members of society, but expanding Social Security doesn't help the middle class very much. Social Security is an entitlement, which redistributes savings based on income. This may be a worthy goal in and of itself, but it is not the focus of our plan.

In contrast to Social Security, the Retirement Savings Plan creates Guaranteed Retirement Accounts, where you get back what you put in, plus investment earnings. These accounts build on the money people put into their own accounts, giving back even more.

Second, unlike Social Security, GRAs depend on actual cash in each person's individually owned account. Because it is real capital that can be invested well, the higher returns fund a lot of the future needs without requiring larger contributions or adding to the deficit.

Since Social Security is an unfunded, pay-as-you-go plan, it cannot do this.

Third, increasing Social Security would mean raising taxes or increasing the deficit. Under the GRA model, employees would be placing their own money in their own account. For employers, their contribution would be offset by the savings from no longer having to administer retirement plans.

Finally, on a political level, an expansion of Social Security would also be difficult to implement. It is such a fraught issue that both sides are dug in with regard to their respective positions.

Is there a role for myRA accounts under the Retirement Savings Plan?

Yes. As currently structured, the myRA program is limited to small amounts (less than $15,000). That is not nearly enough to fund a secure retirement.

However, the myRA program is a good option for people seeking to establish a rainy day fund. It could coexist well with the Retirement Savings Plan, where savings are protected until retirement. Coupled with the GRA, the myRA program is beneficial, since people won't be able to withdraw from their GRA in case of an emergency.

Won't the principal guarantee put taxpayers on the hook if the financial markets crash like they did in 2008?

The cost to the government for the principal guarantee is very small.[61] In fact, no professionally managed pension fund has failed to generate a return over any 25-year period.

The guarantee exists to place a floor beneath every account. The guarantee is such that over a 45-year life-span of the GRA, workers at the end will have accumulated a credit toward their annuitization with an average return of no less than their principal contribution. This minimum return would be utilized solely for computation of their annuity payments on the date they retire, when their GRA rolls over into an annuity. Accordingly, we believe that it is very unlikely that the guarantee will ever cost the government much, and it should have *de minimis* actual economic value (see appendix B). However, if even this modest cost is not something legislators want to bear, GRA holders could pay a small insurance premium, like bank depositors pay on savings accounts.

In any event, regardless of the likelihood of this minimum compounded return ever coming into play, the guarantee will not affect the portfolio risk and return, because the portfolio would be managed by independent managers without regard to the guarantee. Instead, the guarantee would be part of the government's calculation of minimum annuity amounts only when the account is terminated on retirement.

Acknowledgments

WE WOULD LIKE TO THANK PETER ROSE, CHRISTINE Anderson, and Will Pollock for their invaluable research, editing, and encouragement throughout this process. Pete Peterson is an inspiration who proves that anyone's voice can make a difference, and that business leaders have an obligation to help solve society's problems. Neera Tanden got it all started by asking us to do a policy speech in Washington, DC, around a big new idea.

Jeffrey Nussbaum, Michael Flynn, and Adam Talbot contributed their policy backgrounds and expert writing skills to refining the plan. Bridget Fisher at the New School was indispensable in connecting this book to those determined to advance a constructive national plan for retirement security.

Throughout this process, we have been fortunate to meet and speak with leading economists—including Erskine Bowles, Austan Goolsbee, Glenn Hubbard, Alan Krueger, Alicia Munnell, Larry Summers, and Robert Rubin—and with elected officials from across the political spectrum. Republicans and Democrats alike have expressed their determination to find common ground for solving the retirement crisis, and we are profoundly grateful for their commitment to this cause.

We also want to recognize the countless Americans who are strug-gling to do the right thing in a broken system—the employers who do everything they can to provide retirement savings support for their staff, and the employees who work, on average, more hours per week, weeks per year, and years per lifetime than workers in most other wealthy nations. These dedicated men and women deserve a better retirement system—one where their money works as hard as they do to guarantee a secure retirement.

The Budgetary Cost of a GRA

THE RETIREMENT SAVINGS PLAN IS DESIGNED TO BE essentially deficit-neutral; over time, it has the potential to save taxpayers money. This appendix explains how we would achieve these savings.

Government Retirement Spending: The Current System

First, consider what the government already spends on retirement. Right now, the federal government spends $120 billion each year (and state governments spend an additional $20 billion) to incentivize retirement savings. So while most savers are falling behind under this current system, it's not because the government isn't spending enough. The problem is in how the spending is allocated.

These retirement incentives are structured as a tax preference against income for retirement contributions. As currently constructed, however, these benefits are top-heavy and regressive. Seventy percent of current government spending goes toward the highest-earning 20 percent of savers, and that does little to help the savers most in need.

There are four reasons for this imbalance:

1. The vast majority of people earning below the median income level contribute either nothing or very little to retirement savings and therefore receive few of the current tax benefits.

2. High-income savers are more likely to contribute the maximum allowable amount every year and therefore maximize their tax benefits. If they are over age 50, the maximum is $24,000. Under 50, the maximum amount of tax-qualified savings is $18,000. Today, someone over 50 in the top income bracket saving the maximum gets an implicit tax subsidy of $9,480 just on the taxes saved on this contribution.

3. The savers who contribute more are also likely to have higher marginal tax rates, meaning that every pretax dollar they contribute gets more of a subsidy than a dollar saved by a low-income individual.

4. High-income savers are generally the only ones for whom itemizing deductions (such as retirement savings) makes sense.

Tax Benefits under the Retirement Savings Plan

The Retirement Savings Plan would redirect this existing retirement spending, producing outcomes that are both more equitable and more effective for *all* retirement savers.

First, we shift these existing tax breaks toward a universal, refundable tax credit. For example, someone over 50 in the top income bracket would see a reduction in their tax subsidy from today's rate of $9,480 to $1,829 under our plan. By dividing these tax breaks—more than $120 billion—among the anticipated pool of workers covered by a GRA plan, we can give every worker an annual tax credit of up to $600. This covers the entire 1.5 percent savings mandate for nearly everyone earning below median salary, meaning tens of millions of workers will be covered without impacting the budget.

Second, any worker whose 1.5 percent contribution adds up to more than $600 could then deduct the additional required contribution from his or her taxes. For instance, a worker earning $80,000 per year would make a mandated contribution of $1,200. Of that contribution, $600 would be returned in a tax credit, and the remaining $600 would be tax-deductible.

This approach will likely be virtually revenue-neutral or -positive in the short run and potentially would save the government substantial amounts over the long term. Consider four additional reasons why:

- First, larger retirement nest eggs mean fewer seniors in poverty. This will lessen the federal spending burden on comparatively expensive programs like Medicaid, public housing, SNAP, SSI, and other assistance programs.

- Second, when savers reach retirement, their savings are treated as taxable income, just as in the current system. A larger savings pool means higher tax yields when compared to the status quo.

- Third, individuals who earn under $40,000 will not be able to claim the full $600 tax credit. For a saver earning $30,000 a year, for instance, 1.5 percent of income is only $450. They will therefore get their "free" contribution through a $450 tax credit, leaving $150 unclaimed.

- Fourth, because the deduction cap is 1.5 percent of income up to $250,000, the highest-income Americans will be entitled a smaller tax deferment than under the current system—even as the vast majority of Americans receive greater benefits. The maximum credit plus deduction under the plan will be $3,750 as compared to a maximum deduction of $18,000 to 401(k) plans ($24,000 for a person over age 50).

A Clear Improvement on the Status Quo

To understand how this system improves on the status quo, consider four different types of individuals preparing for retirement: a rich individual (making $250,000 a year in gross income), an individual in the top half of the income bracket (making $80,000), a near-median earner (making $40,000), and a minimum wage worker (making $20,000).

Under this scenario, our **affluent savers** (those earning $250,000) receive the $600 credit toward their $3,750 contribution and also a tax deduction (at a tax rate of 39 percent) for the rest of their $3,150 in required savings. The plan gives them $367 more total savings than the current plan if they saved only 1.5 percent. But that is misleading; the GRA plan will take away most tax benefits from the affluent, since most affluent people contribute a lot more than $3,750.

For our **savers in the top half of the income bracket**, 1.5 percent of income is $1,200 per year. Under our plan, this saver would receive total tax benefits of $798. This is a better deal than this saver gets under current law, where she or he would receive only $396 in tax benefits for saving $1,200. Under the RSP, she or he gets $402 more.

For the **near-median earner** ($40,000), 1.5 percent of income is $600—fully covered by the $600 tax credit. This is a much better deal than the current system, where this saver's tax benefit would have been worth only $162.

Finally, for the **minimum wage worker**, at $20,000 per year, 1.5 percent of income is $300. So for this saver, the tax credit is $300. Again, this is a much better deal than the current model, where this minimum wage worker would receive only $30 in tax deferment if he or she were able to save $300.

What is the total benefit to the contributor?

The total benefit is the tax deduction for contributions above $600 and the $600 gift (in the case of lower-income worker, the gift is $600 or 1.5 percent of income, whatever is less). For the top earner, their total gift from the government is $1,829; for the $80,000/year earner, $798; for the $40,000/year earner, $600; and for the $20,000/year earner, $300.

Here are the detailed calculations. For the top earner, their total benefit was $600 plus the tax break on the extra that they are required to contribute to their GRA—$3,150—which is $1,229 ($3,150 times their current tax rate of 39 percent). The total gift is the tax break on the contributions made after the $600 gift, $1,229, plus the $600, or $1,829.

The total subsidy from the government for the $80,000 earner is less but a larger portion of their total income. They are required to contribute $1,200. They receive a $600 credit from the government and therefore must contribute an extra $600. The tax break for them on this $600 is their tax rate, 33 percent, times the $600, which is $198. They get this $198 break on the taxes, and they get a $600 credit, so the total benefit from the government is $798.

Take the $40,000 earner. They are required to contribute $600, which is their required GRA contribution of 1.5 percent of their $40,000 earnings. Since they receive a $600 credit, which completely covers their GRA contribution, they do not contribute anything over and above the $600, which means they do not receive a tax deduction. Their total benefit from the government is $600.

	Affluent	Top-Half Income Bracket	Near-Median	Minimum Wage
Gross income	$250,000	$80,000	$40,000	$20,000
Required contribution	0.015	0.015	0.015	0.015
Contribution credited to a person's GRA	$3,750	$1,200	$600	$300
Credit under the tax deferment model	$600	$600	$600	$300
Required contribution after the credit	$3,150	$600	$0	$0
Tax rate	0.39	0.33	0.27	0.1
AGI	$246,850	$79,400	$40,000	$20,000
Tax bill without special contribution	$97,500	$26,400	$10,800	$2,000

	Affluent	Top-Half Income Bracket	Near-Median	Minimum Wage
New tax bill after GRA contribution is deducted	$96,272	$26,202	$10,800	$2,000
Deferment under current law (assuming savings of 1.5% of income)	$1,463	$396	$162	$30
Deferment under GRA (for savings of 1.5% of income)	$1,829	$798	$600	$300
Total benefit is the tax deduction for contributions above $600 and $600 (or 1.5% of income, whatever is less)	$1,829	$798	$600	$300

Conclusion

GRAs aren't just a great deal for savers, they're a better bargain for the American taxpayer.

By moving to a GRA system, our country will solve a looming retirement crisis—while mitigating the fiscal risk that comes from an elderly population at higher risk of poverty than at any point in the past sixty years.

As a nation, we're going to need to care for these senior citizens one way or another, and this option makes that possible without additional spending or expanding the budget deficit. Most important, it is a plan that preserves retirees' dignity while strengthening our country.

The Cost of a Government Guarantee

In order to test the potential costs of a government principal protection guarantee, which guarantees that each saver gets back at least as much as they contribute, we constructed a series of simulations to analyze future return scenarios. This research found unequivocally that a government principal protection guarantee poses no significant financial risk to taxpayers.

In particular, this analysis revealed three key facts:

1. It is extremely unlikely that the principal protection government guarantee would ever be triggered. In fact, there has never been a 40-year period in recent history where the guarantee would have been called upon.

2. Even if it is triggered, the costs would be minimal. They could be easily covered by a very small onetime upfront fee of $15 on each account.

3. Once the program is past its transitional implementation stage, maintaining the guarantee will be simple and almost certainly costless. In our analysis, the principal protection guarantee is likely to cost the government only while the program is being put into place—and these scenarios are themselves highly unlikely. These potential costs then become even less likely with each passing year.

In this appendix, we take those findings one at a time.

1. It is extremely unlikely that the principal protection guarantee will be triggered.

To understand why the **principal protection** guarantee is a safe bet, begin by considering how the accounts are structured. Workers cannot withdraw funds until retirement, and the accounts are pooled and invested in balanced portfolios of investments that are not correlated with each other. These larger, pooled investment accounts would have lower fees and offer advantages of scale, including better diversification options and access to alternative investments. As everything is aggregated on a national scale, the risks are diffused as well.

To measure the size and likelihood of risks posed to taxpayers, we constructed a series of Monte Carlo simulations. Our analysis found that the probability of the guarantee being called after 40 years ranges from 0.1 to 0.4 percent (depending on the specifications used, which are described in the next paragraph). And in every one of these cases, the guarantee shortfall could be met via the fee reserve (see below).

In terms of the model specification, we used historical pension fund returns from 1945 to 2015 to fit two distributions: Gaussian and noncentral t-distribution. The normal (Gaussian) distribution is standard for modeling, and the noncentral t-distribution allows for fat-tailed downside risk. We also tested autoregressive and generalized autoregressive conditional heteroskedasticity (GARCH) model specifications, but found they had worse model comparison scores (AIC/BIC) and insignificant p-values. In all models, we combine historical fits with expectations of future returns.

Our baseline scenario is that Guaranteed Retirement Accounts (GRA) will earn an average of 6.75 percent over the next 40 years with a standard deviation of returns of 11 percent. To put this in perspective, since 1945, pension fund returns averaged 8.7 percent with a standard deviation of 11.4 percent; since 1980, returns averaged 10.2 percent with a standard deviation of 9.8 percent; since 1990, returns averaged 8.9 percent with a 10.3 percent standard deviation.[62]

In fact, there has never been a 40-year period in recent history where a principal protection guarantee would have been triggered. Rolling 40-year average annual returns on pension funds have ranged from 7 percent to 10 percent in every period since the one ending in 1985—meaning even a guarantee as high as 6.5 percent would never have been called.

Even for the period from 1969 to 2008, which ended in a global financial crisis, GRA savers would have still earned close to an 8 percent return. Portfolio values did decrease by 25 percent in 2008, but this only moved the average return down by 1.5 percent. Pension funds would have had to lose 88 percent in 2008 in order to push lifetime average returns negative.

2. Even if the principal protection guarantee is triggered, the costs will be minimal and easily covered by a very small fee on all GRAs.

All the same, it's relatively straightforward to calculate what the costs would be in the unlikely event that the principal protection guarantee is triggered.

Consider a saver earning $52,000 annually. (These earnings lie between the median and average annual earnings of a full time American worker.) If we assume a 40-year career, and 2 percent annual wage growth, this person would eventually contribute $98,000 into their GRA, and the expected portfolio value, assuming a 6.75 percent annual return, would be $393,000 after that period.

In order to insure against the extremely unlikely event that the GRA has negative returns over 40 years, the government could impose a onetime fee of $15 for each new GRA member. This is the present expected value of the principal protection guarantee. The proposal doesn't necessarily recommend the levee; the calculation merely illustrates how low the theoretical cost of the guarantee really is.

Through a small fee like this, the reserve fund would receive $2.4 billion in the first year and $8 billion over the first 40 years of the program. Accrued at a long-term, risk-free rate, the reserve fund would be worth $21 billion in 40 years, which is large enough to cover over half of all possible loss scenarios in our Monte Carlo simulations—bringing the probability of taxpayers being forced to step in down to 0.001 percent.

3. Once the program is mature, maintaining the guarantee will be simple and almost certainly costless.

The risk of this reserve fund falling short is not evenly distributed over the life of the program, either. In fact, the only scenarios in which it falls short occur during the transitional first years after the GRA system is instituted—but even in these very unlikely scenarios, the exposure is small.

In this short-term scenario, claims would be smaller for a simple reason: people would have made fewer contributions over a shorter time frame. If a GRA had been introduced in 2004, for example, 1.7 million workers would have claimed benefits under the guarantee in 2008 (see below). However, the shortfall would have been relatively small—just over $1 billion—because the median participant would have lost $660 of the total $4,800 invested.

Cost of principal protection guarantee for the cohort retiring in 2008 (1.7 million people) by hypothetical GRA starting year

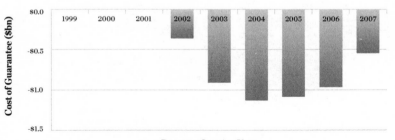

Program Starting Year

Source: Keith Blackwell and Teresa Ghilarducci (2016) "The Cost of a Guaranteed Return." Schwartz Center for Economic Policy Analysis and Department of Economics, The New School for Social Research, forthcoming working paper series 2016-2.

Similarly, if a GRA were instituted today, risks associated with large drops in the market value of worker portfolios such as the one that occurred in 2008 would be greatest in the first five years, but then begin to wane (see below). Even assuming a 6.75 percent average annual return followed by a 25 percent decrease in 2021, the median individual retiring that year would have a portfolio that would only be down $1,100.

In this scenario, the guarantee's total cost would be $2.5 billion, which is less than the value of fees collected up to that point. In *every* scenario—including a 25 percent drop in the first year of implementation—the buffer would be large enough to cover the losses without the government needing to intervene.

Projected cost of guarantee starting 2016 for each cohort if there are 6.75 percent annual returns until retirement year and then a 25 percent decline

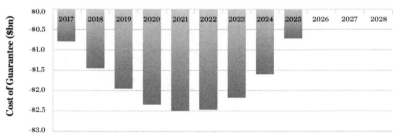

Year of 25% decline in portfolio value

Source: Keith Blackwell and Teresa Ghilarducci (2016) "The Cost of a Guaranteed Return." Schwartz Center for Economic Policy Analysis and Department of Economics, The New School for Social Research, forthcoming working paper series 2016-2.

Additional Research: The Low Risk Potential of Guarantees

It may be tempting to fall back on standard financial engineering textbook approaches to costing guarantees—which tend to project higher prices through option pricing techniques. However, while option pricing techniques are appropriate for finding the price of an option purchased in financial markets, this approach is not appropriate to estimate the cost of a government guarantee, because the US government doesn't function like an investment bank does.

- The government is not resource- (balance sheet) constrained, nor is it subject to the same continuous mark-to-market rules.

- The government can bear long-term risks more easily than an individual investment bank.

- A government guarantee on a retirement account is not a pure financial transaction between independent market participants. A government guarantee is a transaction between all workers facilitated by the government.

- As such, the option price is not the "value of resources forgone" by society, as claimed by a 2016 Brookings Institution paper.[63]

A wide body of research supports our conclusions. Alicia Munnell et al. (2009) evaluated the cost of a guarantee and found no significant risk to a 2–3 percent nominal return guarantee.[64] Stubbs (2012) modeled a 3.5 percent guarantee using Monte Carlo simulations and 80 years of market returns. He found little or no risk of not earning a

3.5 percent real return on a balanced portfolio, even though it is well above the RSP's guaranteed level. [65]

Olivia Mitchell (2015) claims a return guarantee is irresponsible, but her subject is meaningfully different from the GRA system. [66] Mitchell's research refers to guarantees of pure equity portfolios and involves guarantees much higher than our proposal. In fact, Mitchell and LaChance (2002) argue the cost of providing principal protection for a 50/50 equity/bond split portfolio, a portfolio with similar volatility profile to a pension fund, would be less than $1 per account. [67]

Conclusion

In summary, the risks of a government principal protection guarantee for individual retirement accounts are exceedingly minimal, while the peace of mind it would provide is crucial. In every scenario, the GRA system is a cost-effective way to guarantee a secure pension for every American worker.

We acknowledge Keith Blackwell, economics graduate student at the New School for Social Research, for his invaluable help in writing this appendix.

GRAs vs.
Other Policy Solutions

In recognition of the oncoming retirement crisis, numerous policy proposals have been put forth at both the state and federal levels.[68] In 2009, the Obama administration proposed an IRA that did not advance in Congress. Meanwhile, over 14 state governments are considering various types of retirement plans for private sector workers.

Momentum and innovation to solve inadequate retirement plan coverage at the state level indicates the need for a federal solution. As in past policymaking, such as Social Security, state innovation often informs and shapes federal programs.

Obama Administration's Auto IRA

This proposal aimed to benefit workers without access to a retirement plan at work. It would require employers that do not already offer a retirement plan to enroll their employees in a direct-deposit IRA account compatible with existing direct deposit payroll systems.[69] Three percent of each paycheck would be deposited into a Roth IRA, in which contributions are made with after-tax dollars. Withdrawals from the Roth IRA would be tax-free for account holders age 59.5, or older if the account was held for at least five years.[70]

Obama's Auto IRA initiative also proposed to expand retirement savings incentives for working families by modifying the existing saver's credit to provide a onetime 50 percent match on the first $1,000 of retirement savings for families who earn less than $65,000. The credit would have been fully refundable to ensure that savings incentives are fair to all workers.[71]

Advantages

- Those who make contributions to Auto IRA accounts may be eligible to benefit from the saver's credit, which is a contribution for low- and middle-income workers who save for retirement. In this case, the government would pay part of the cost of the saver's contribution to the IRA.

- Automatic enrollment is an effective means for workers to save for retirement, and this proposal attempts to bring more workers into retirement savings programs.

Disadvantages

- The proposal did not advance in Congress.

- Employees can opt out and withdraw from accounts before retirement, both of which result in suboptimal retirement savings.

- The saver's credit requires over $50 billion if it is refundable and income limits are increased.[72]

Obama Administration's MyRA

After the Obama Administration's original Auto IRA was rejected, the United States Treasury developed a retirement account plan entitled "myRA." It is a type of Roth IRA, where individual savers can contribute up to $5,500 annually into myRA accounts.

These contributions are then invested in US government securities, which averaged an annual return of 3.19 percent over the ten-year period ending December 2014.[73] Since a government bond guarantees a saver cannot lose money, the return will not be high.[74] Employers are not required to directly administer or contribute to the accounts, only to facilitate them by deducting contributions from paychecks through direct deposit.

To avoid competition with financial services firms, the US Treasury directly administers the myRA accounts (in cooperation with a private-sector bank) when they are small and turns them over to private-sector IRAs once the account balance is greater than the $15,000 maximum amount, or after thirty years.[75]

Advantages

- The myRA accounts aim to increase retirement savings.

- People contributing to myRAs may be eligible for the saver's credit.

- Workers are shielded from investment and market risks by investing in US Treasury securities.

Disadvantages

- MyRA accounts are voluntary, for both the employer to offer and the employee to participate in. Unless there is auto-enrollment, people are not likely to enroll, especially low- and middle-income taxpayers.[76]

- The maximum contribution cap of $15,000 may inhibit more savings, and the commercial IRAs to which they will be converted have high fees.

- The return rate on US government securities is secure but low and may not beat inflation. [77]

- There are no provisions for annuities.

- Overall, myRA accounts are a first step to expand retirement savings, but without automatic enrollment and given the low cap, they will not be an effective way to increase savings enough to fund lifelong benefits.

The Secure Choice Retirement Savings Program

Secure Choice Pensions (SCPs) are state-level proposals aimed to provide retirement security for workers by requiring certain employers to make payroll deductions on behalf of their employees for savings in Roth IRAs. [78] A handful of states—Illinois, Massachusetts, Oregon, California, Maryland, and Connecticut—are at various stages of researching and implementing automatic payroll deduction retirement plans. Participants would be fully vested in their accrued benefits immediately, and the amounts contributed plus earnings would be overseen by an independent board of trustees who administer the plan.

Advantages

- SCPs are being proposed and considered across the country[79] and help millions of private sector workers without access to any kind of pension plan.

- SCPs could provide guaranteed minimum retirement income (with the possibility for additional earnings) and a life annuity benefit, although none of the Secure Choice plans currently do so.

- If participants were provided with a pooled investment option, they could get higher returns with less risk because of the advantages of economies of scale in obtaining low fees and low risk from diversification.

Disadvantages

- In all of the Secure Choice models, as with the myRA plan, workers can opt out of an individual account and are likely to do so if they require short-term funds for daily financial struggles.

- None of the models have a presumed annuity payout.

AFSCME Retirement Program

The State Supplemental Social Security Act proposed by the American Federation of State, County, and Municipal Employees (AFSCME) proposes a mandated and advance-funded supplement to Social Security managed by the state.

This proposal would have states raise payroll taxes to pay for a benefit computed using the Social Security actuarial methodology. Employees must have 40 quarters of covered service to qualify for any benefit, and if they move out of state, they will have both their and their employer's contributions returned after age 62. [80]

Advantages

- This is an ambitious proposal that entails the federal government eventually mandating a supplement to Social Security.

Disadvantages

- The proposal received little support in state legislatures, which found Secure Choice proposals that do not raise taxes were more popular.

- Despite being the purest form of filling the void left by the erosion of defined benefit plans, the corporate business structure no longer supports the defined benefit model.

AARP's "Work and Save"

AARP's "Work and Save" proposal aims to support businesses in creating private retirement savings accounts for employees based on the model of 529 plans. These plans would be authorized by the state, run by the private sector, and professionally managed.

Work and Save seeks to support five main principles of a retirement program: financial freedom, voluntary participation, portability, saving taxpayer dollars, and no risk.

The Work and Save program allows money saved by participants to travel with the owner, provides tax advantages to enrollees, is available to everyone—including small businesses and low-income employees—and has a low cost to taxpayers and participants.

Advantages

- The Work and Save proposal has support from a variety of aging, human services, business, and labor groups across the country.

- More than a dozen states have considered legislation of this kind. Massachusetts, California, and Oregon were the first to enact legislation.

- AARP has presented surveys showing support for such a plan among a majority of workers who do not have access to any kind of retirement plan.

Disadvantages

- The program is voluntary, which leaves it impractical and vulnerable to a lack of participation and withdrawals.

Working Longer

People facing inadequate retirement income often rely on working longer as a solution. However, they also face an increasingly unfriendly job market as they get older. Employers often prefer hiring younger workers, leaving older workers to face longer periods of unemployment. Additionally, poor health, either one's own or a spouse's, can make it impossible to work. Altogether, older workers expecting to work longer often end up retiring earlier than planned.

According to EBRI's confidence survey, workers expect to retire at age 65.[81] However, the average age of retirement is much lower: about age 62.[82] From 2010 to 2015 the number of retirees who said they retired earlier than expected went up 9 percent. This is because of poor health—affecting themselves or their spouse —or because they were laid off, not promoted, or not trained.[83]

Most of those faced with the reality of not being able to retire due to inadequate savings report that they plan to work longer or "die at their desk." The unpleasant realities of the labor market for older workers do not justify dependence on employment until 70 years of age to maintain living standards into retirement. This includes some inconvenient facts: many older people can't work because they care for fragile spouses or family members; older workers face high rates of long-term unemployment and falling wages; age discrimination is a persistent problem; and the pace and technical content of work continue to increase.[84]

The share of older workers who say they have physically demanding jobs is increasing, while the share of jobs reported as easy is falling. The incidence of requirements for stooping, bending, and using keen eyesight and intense concentration is increasing.

After workers reach ages 55–69, they experience a decline in earnings regardless of education, as they are overlooked for promotions and on-the-job training. This reminds us that work in old age is not the solution to the retirement crisis.

Advantages

- The worker receives more income and continues working a job that interests him/her.

Disadvantages

- Working in old age degrades the health of the worker.

- Workers cannot take care of dependent family members.

- High rates of long-term unemployment and falling wages are prevalent among elderly workers.

- Older workers face age discrimination from employers.

First published in "Now Is the Time to Add Retirement Accounts to Social Security: The Guaranteed Retirement Account Proposal" (2015).

Notes

1. Ghilarducci, T. and H. E. James. "A Smarter Plan to Make Retirement Savings Last." *The New York Times*, January 1, 2016. http://www.nytimes.com/2016/01/02/opinion/a-smarterplan-to-make-retirement-savings-last.html.

2. Holland, K. "For Millions, 401(k) Plans Have Fallen Short." CNBC.com, March 23, 2015. http://www.cnbc.com/2015/03/20/l-it-the-401k-is-a-failure.html.

3. Employee Benefit Research Institute. "FAQs about Benefits—Retirement Issues." Accessed May 20, 2016. https://www.ebri.org/publications/benfaq/index.cfm?fa=retfaq14.

4. Saad-Lessler, J., T. Ghilarducci, and K. Bahn. "Are U.S. Workers Ready for Retirement? Trends in Plan Sponsorship, Participation, and Preparedness." Schwartz Center for Economic Policy Analysis, The New School. http://www.economicpolicyresearch.org/images/docs/research/retirement_security/Are_US_Workers_Ready_for_Retirement.pdf.

5. Saad-Lessler, J., T. Ghilarducci, and K. Bahn. "Are U.S. Workers Ready for Retirement? Trends in Plan Sponsorship, Participation, and Preparedness." *Journal of Pension Benefits*, Ferenczy Benefits Law Center (Winter 2015): 25–39. http://ssrn.com/abstract=2604299.

6. Smith, M. "The Retirement Gamble." *Frontline*, April 23, 2013. http://www.pbs.org/wgbh/frontline/film/retirement-gamble/transcript/.

7. Costa, S. "Health Buzz: Americans Are Living Longer. " *U.S. News & World Report*, January 21, 2016. http://health.usnews.com/health-news/health-wellness/articles/2016-01-21/americans-are-living-longer.

8. Miller, K., D. Madland, and C. E. Weller. "The Reality of the Retirement Crisis." Center for American Progress, January 26, 2015. https://www .americanprogress.org/issues/economy/report/2015/01/26/105394 /the-reality-of-the-retirement-crisis.html.

9. Aon Hewitt. "The 2012 Real Deal Highlights." Aon.com, 2012. http://www .aon.com/attachments/human-capital-consulting/The_2012_Real_Deal _Highlights.pdf.

10. Oakley, D. and K. Keanelly. "Retirement Security 2015: Roadmap for Policy Makers: Americans' Views of the Retirement Crisis." National Institute for Retirement Security, March 2015. http:// www.nirsonline.org/index.php ?option=content&task=view&id=881.html.

11. Ghilarducci, T. and Z. Knauss. "More Middle Class Workers Will Be Poor Retirees." Schwartz Center for Economic Policy Analysis and Department of Economics, The New School for Social Research, Policy Note Series, 2015. http://www.economicpolicyresearch.org/images/docs/retirement_ security _background/Downward_Mobility.pdf.

12. Aon Hewitt. "The 2012 Real Deal Highlights." Aon.com, 2012. http://www .aon.com/attachments/human-capital-consulting/The_2012_Real_Deal _Highlights.pdf.

13. Fernandes, D. "A Warning on Realities of Work, Retirement." *The Boston Globe*, November 30, 2014. https:// www.bostonglobe.com/business /2014/11/30/economist-sounds-warning-reality-retirement.

14. Center on Budget and Policy Priorities. "Policy Basics: Top Ten Facts about Social Security." August 13, 2015. http://www.cbpp.org/research /social-security/policy-basics-top-ten-facts-about-social-security.

15. Lieber, R. "Getting a Reverse Mortgage, but Not from a Celebrity." *The New York Times*, June 10, 2016. http://www.nytimes.com/2016/06/11 /your-money/getting-a-reverse-mortgage-but-not-from-a-celebrity.html.

16. Tong, S. "Father of Modern 401(k) Says It Fails Many Americans." Marketplace .org, June 13, 2013. http://www. marketplace.org/2013/06/13/sustainability /consumed/father-modern-401k-says-it-fails-many-americans.html.

17. Anderson, T. "The Surprising Origins of Your 401(k)." Nasdaq.com, July 8, 2013. http://www.nasdaq.com/article/the-surprising-origins-of-your-401k -cm258685.

18. Tong, S. "Father of Modern 401(k) Says It Fails Many Americans." Marketplace, June 13, 2013. www.marketplace.org/2013/06/13 /sustainability/consumed/father-modern-401k-says-it-fails-many-americans.

19. Holland, K. "For Millions, 401(k) Plans Have Fallen Short." CNBC.com, March 23, 2015. http://www.cnbc.com/2015/03/20/1-it-the-401k-is-a -failure.html.

20. Olshan, J. "'Father' of the 401(k)'s Tough Love." Marketwatch, November 22, 2011. http://blogs.marketwatch.com/encore/2011/11/22/father-of-the -401ks-tough-love/.

21. Kujawa, P. "A 'Father's' Wisdom: An Interview with Ted Benna." Workforce.com, January 20, 2012. http://www.workforce.com/articles/a-father-s -wisdom-an-interview-with-ted-benna.

22. Munnell, A., A. Webb, and F. Golub-Sass. "The National Retirement Risk Index: An Update." Center for Retirement Research at Boston College, October 2012. http://crr.bc.edu/briefs/the-national-retirement-risk-index -an-update/.

23. Miller, K., D. Madland, and C. E. Weller. "The Reality of the Retirement Crisis." Center for American Progress, January 26, 2015. https://www .americanprogress.org/issues/economy/report/2015/01/26/105394/ the -reality-of-the-retirement-crisis.html.

24. Aon Hewitt. "The 2012 Real Deal Highlights." Aon.com, 2012. http://www .aon.com/attachments/human-capital-consulting/The_2012_Real_Deal _Highlights.pdf.

25. United States Government Accountability Office. "Retirement Security: Most Households Approaching Retirement Have Low Savings." Report to the Ranking Member, Subcommittee on Primary Health and Retirement Security, Committee on Health, Education, Labor, and Pensions, U.S. Senate, May 2015. http://www.gao.gov/assets/680/670153.pdf.

26. Pramuk, J. "New York Fed: Household Debt at Highest Level Since 2010."

CNBC.com, November 19, 2015. http://www. CNBC.com/2015/11/19/new
-york-fed-household-debt-at-highest-level-since-2010.html.

27. Quoted in Olson, E. "For Many Women, Adequate Pensions Are Still a Far
    Reach." *The New York Times*, June 3, 2016. http://www.nytimes.com/2016
    /06/04/your-money/for-many-women-adequate-pensions-are-still-a-far
    -reach.html.

28. Vasilogambros, M. "Americans Want to Save More Money. They Just Can't."
    The Atlantic, April 21, 2014. http://www.theatlantic.com/business/archive
    /2014/04/americans-want-to-save-more-money-they-just-cant/425376/.

29. Board of Governors of the Federal Reserve System. "Report on the Economic
    Well-Being of U.S. Households in 2014." May 2015. https://www
    .federalreserve.gov/econresdata/2014-report-economic-well-being-us
    -households-201505.pdf.

30. Summers, N. "In Australia, Retirement Savings Done Right." Bloomberg.com,
    May 30, 2013. http://www.bloomberg.com/news/articles/2013-05-30
    /in-australia-retirement-saving-done-right.

31. Schrager, A. "Behind the Venture Capital Boom: Public Pensions." Bloomberg
    .com, September 23, 2014. http://www.bloomberg.com/news/articles
    /2014-09-23/are-public-pensions-inflating-a-venture-capital-bubble.

32. Ghilarducci, T. and Zachary Knauss. "More Middle Class Workers Will Be Poor
    Retirees." Schwartz Center for Economic Policy Analysis and Department of
    Economics, The New School for Social Research, Policy Note Series, 2015.
    http://www.economicpolicyresearch.org/images/docs
    /retirement_ security_background/Downward_Mobility.pdf.

33. National Institute on Aging. "Growing Older in America: The Health and
    Retirement Study." U.S. Department of Health & Human Services, 2007.
    https://d2cauhfh6h4x0p.cloudfront.net/s3fs-public/health_and
    _retirement_study_0.pdf.

34. Munnell, A., A. Webb, and F. Golub-Sass. "The National Retirement Risk Index:
    An Update." Center for Retirement Research at Boston College, October 2012.
    http://crr.bc.edu/briefs/the-national-retirement-risk-index
    -an-update/.

35. Epperson, S. "Annuities for Retirement: Good or Bad Idea?" CNBC.com, October 24, 2014. http://www.cnbc. com/2014/10/24/annuities-for -retirement-good-or-bad-idea.html.

36. Roosevelt, F. D. *Public Papers of the President of the United States*, Vol. 9. Washington, DC: Office of the Federal Register, National Archives and Records Administration, 1940.

37. Aon Hewitt. "Customize DC Investments for Participant Success." Aon.com, July 2015. http://www.aon.com/attachments/human-capital-consulting /custom-dc-investments-for-participant-success-wp-july2015.pdf.

38. Ibid.

39. Ghilarducci, T., B. Fisher, and Z. Knauss. "Now Is the Time to Add Retirement Accounts to Social Security: The Guaranteed Retirement Account Proposal." Schwartz Center for Economic Policy Analysis and Department of Economics, The New School for Social Research, 2015.

40. Nyce, S. and B. J. Quade. "Annuities and Retirement Happiness." Willis Towers Watson, 2012. https://www.towerswatson.com/en-US/Insights /Newsletters/Americas/insider/2012/Annuities-and-Retirement-Happiness.

41. Panis, C. "Annuities and Retirement Satisfaction." Labor and Population Program Working Paper 03-17. RAND, 2003.

42. Bender, K. and N. Jivan. "What Makes Retirees Happy?" An Issue in Brief 28. Boston College, Center for Retirement Research, 2005.

43. Flavelle, C. "The Inequality of Retirement Anxiety." *Bloomberg View*, 2015.

44. Eisenberg, R. "To Solve the U.S. Retirement Crisis, Look to Australia." *Forbes*, August 19, 2013. http://www.forbes.com/sites/nextavenue /2013/08/19/to-solve-the-u-s-retirement-crisis-look-to-australia /#d03acaf445f6.

45. Summers, N. "In Australia, Retirement Savings Done Right." Bloomberg.com, May 30, 2013. http://www.bloomberg.com/news/articles/2013-05-30 /in-australia-retirement-saving-done-right.

46. Eisenberg, R. "To Solve the U.S. Retirement Crisis, Look to Australia."
    Forbes, August 19, 2013. http://www.forbes.com/sites/nextavenue
    /2013/08/19/to-solve-the-u-s-retirement-crisis-look-to-australia
    /#d03acaf445f6.

47. Shorten, B. "20 Years of Superannuation." Address to ASFA Superannuation
    Guarantee Dinner. Australian Treasury Portfolio Ministers, August 16, 2011.
    http://ministers.treasury.gov.au/DisplayDocs.aspx?doc=speeches/2011/028
    .htm&pageID=005&min=brsa&Year=&DocType=1.

48. Power, T. "Liberals Slow Down SG Increase until July 2025." *SuperGuide*,
    January 12, 2016.

49. The Association of Superannuation Funds of Australia. "Superannuation
    Statistics." 2015. https://www.superannuation.asn.au/resources
    /superannuation-statistics.

50. Stewart, T. "Super Satisfaction Increasing: Roy Morgan." *Investor Daily*, May
    28, 2015. http://www.investordaily.com.au/superannuation/37615
    -super-satisfaction-increasing-roy-morgan. http://www.superguide.com
    .au/boost-your-superannuation/liberals-sg-lisc.html.

51. Munnell, A., A. Webb, and F. Golub-Sass. "The National Retirement Risk Index:
    An Update." Center for Retirement Research at Boston College, October 2012.
    http://crr.bc.edu/briefs/the-national-retirement-risk-index
    -an-update/.

52. Australian Centre for Financial Studies. "Melbourne Mercer Global Pension
    Index." 2015. http://www. globalpensionindex.com/wp-content/uploads
    /Melbourne-Mercer-Global-Pension-Index-2015-Report-Web.pdf.

53. Ibid.

54. Peltz, J. "Obama Wants to Help California Create More Retirement-Savings
    Accounts." *Los Angeles Times*, July 13, 2015. http://www.latimes.com
    /business/la-fi-0713-obama-retirement-savings-20150713-story.html.

55. Siegel-Bernard, T. "More States Are Initiating Programs to Encourage
    Retirement Savings." *The New York Times*, November 16, 2015. http://www
    .nytimes.com/2015/11/17/your-money/more-states-are-initiating-programs
    -to-encourage-retirement-savings.html.

56. Miller, M. "Can State Auto-IRA Plans Improve Retirement Security?" Retirement Revised, October 24, 2015. http://retirementrevised.com/can -state-auto-ira-plans-improve-retirement-security/.

57. Oakley, D. and K. Keanelly. "Retirement Security 2015: Roadmap for Policy Makers: Americans' Views of the Retirement Crisis." National Institute for Retirement Security, March 2015. http:// www.nirsonline.org/index.php ?option=content&task=view&id=881.html.

58. Riffkin, R. "Americans Settling on Older Retirement Age." Gallup, April 29, 2015. http://www.gallup.com/poll/182939/americans-settling-older -retirement-age.aspx.

59. Jones, J. "More U.S. Nonretirees Expect to Rely on Social Security." Gallup, April 29, 2015. http://www.gallup.com/poll/182921/nonretirees-expect-rely -social-security.aspx.

60. Crowley, J. "Vice Chair Crowley Unveils New, Groundbreaking Plan to Address Savings Crisis in U.S. and Help American Families Save." Keynote at Center for American Progress Action Fund Event, 2015. http://crowley .house.gov/press-release/vice-chair-crowley-unveils-new-groundbreaking -plan-address-savings-crisis-us-and-help.

61. Blackwell, K. and T. Ghilarducci. "The Guarantee's Cost to the Government: SCEPA Policy Brief." Schwartz Center for Economic Policy Analysis, The New School for Social Research, 2016.

62. MSCI Analytics. "InvestorForce Report." MSCI.com. https://www.msci.com /documents/1296102/1636401/InvestorForce_Report.pdf/1b6f2b80-dbfe -4f69-995a-4e2131fbc2fa.

63. Gale, W. G., D. C. John, and B. Kim. "You Get What You Pay For: Guaranteed Returns in Retirement Saving Accounts." Policy Brief. Economic Studies at Brookings, March 2016. http://www.brookings.edu/~/media /research/files/papers/2016/03/14-gale-papers/galejohnkim_ yougetwhatyoupayfor_policybrief_03032016_dp_wg_bk.pdf.

64. Munnell, A. H., A. Golub-Sass, R. W. Kopcke, and A. Webb. "What Does It Cost to Guarantee Returns?" Center for Retirement Research at Boston College, February 2009, No. 9-4. http://crr.bc.edu/wp-content/uploads /2009/02/IB_9-4.pdf.

65. Stubbs, D. M. and N. Rhee. "Can a Publicly Sponsored Retirement Plan for Private Sector Workers Guarantee Benefits at No Risk to the State?" Policy Brief. University of California, Berkeley Center for Labor Research and Education, August 2012. http://laborcenter.berkeley.edu/pdf/2012/ca _guaranteed_retirement_study12.pdf.

66. Mitchell, O. "The Irresponsibility of States Guaranteeing Pension Returns." The Experts Blog. *The Wall Street Journal*, November 5, 2015. http://blogs .wsj.com/experts/2015/11/05/the-irresponsibility-of-states-guaranteeing -pension-returns/.

67. Lachance, M. and O. S. Mitchell. "Understanding Individual Account Guarantees." Working Paper 9195. National Bureau of Economic Research, September 2002. http://www.nber.org/papers/w9195.pdf.

68. Ghilarducci, T., B. Fisher, and Z. Knauss. "Now Is the Time to Add Retirement Accounts to Social Security: The Guaranteed Retirement Account Proposal." Schwartz Center for Economic Policy Analysis and Department of Economics, The New School for Social Research, 2015.

69. The Pew Charitable Trusts. "President Obama's Budget Includes Automatic IRA Proposal and Expansion of Saver's Credit for 401(k)/IRA Savings." Press release, July 21, 2014. http://www.pewtrusts.org/en/about/newsroom /press-releases/0001/01/01/president-obamas-budget-includes-automatic -ira-proposal-and-expansion-of-savers-credit-for-401k-ira-savings.

70. Brandon, E. "New Details of Obama's Automatic IRA Proposal." *U.S. News & World Report*, February 2, 2010. http://money.usnews.com/money/blogs /planning-to-retire/2010/02/02/new-details-of-obamas-automatic-ira -proposal.

71. Executive Office of the President, Office of Management and Budget. "A New Era of Responsibility: Renewing America's Promise." Washington, DC: US Government Printing Office, 2009.

72. Aon Consulting. "Automatic IRA Legislation." Aon.com, September 2010. http://www.aon.com/attachments/auto_ira_sep2010.pdf.

73. "myRA—My Retirement Account: About myRA." 2015. https://myra .treasury.gov.

74. Tergesen, A. "12 Things You Should Know about the myRA." *Marketwatch*, 2015. http://blogs.marketwatch.com/encore/2014/02/04/12-things-savers -should-know-about-the-myra/.

75. Munnell, A. "The myRA Addresses a Serious Problem." *Marketwatch*, February 12, 2014. http://blogs.marketwatch.com/encore/2014/02/12 /the-myra-addresses-a-serious-problem/.

76. Steverman, B. "There's Something about MyRA." Bloomberg.com, 2015.

77. Weltman, B. "Weighing the Pros and Cons of Obama's MyRA." Inc.com, 2015.

78. Kranc, J. "States Move to Implement Retirement Accounts." *Institutional Investor*, February 4, 2015.

79. For information on the progress of state GRAs: http://www.ncpers.org/files /2014_02_20%20NCPERS%20MD%20Testimony_FINAL%20(1).pdf; http://www .usretirementfacts.com/state-activity-2/; http://www.seiu1000.org/sites /main/files/fileattachments/040814_update.pdf.

80. The contributions are returned with the lesser of 5 percent compounded interest or actual returns of the fund from the date the employee first made contributions, through the last day of the month prior to the employee claiming contribution.

81. Employee Benefit Research Institute. "2015 RCS Fact Sheet #2: Expectations about Retirement." Retirement Confidence Survey. EBRI, 2015.

82. Burtless, G. "Can Educational Attainment Explain the Rise in Labor Force Participation at Older Ages?" Center for Retirement Research at Boston College, 2013, 13–33; and Aaron, H. and G. Burtless. *Closing the Deficit: How Much Can Later Retirement Help?* Brookings Institution Press, 2013.

83. Helman, R., C. Copeland, and J. VanDerhei. "The 2015 Retirement Confidence Survey: Having a Retirement Savings Plan a Key Factor in Americans' Retirement Confidence." Issue Brief 413. Employee Benefit Research Institute, 2015.

84. Bonen, A. "Older Workers and Employers' Demands." Policy Note. The New School: Schwartz Center for Economic Policy Analysis, 2013.; Johnson, R., G. Mermin, and M. Resseger. "Employment at Older Ages and the Changing Nature of Work." The Urban Institute, 2007.

About the Authors

 TERESA GHILARDUCCI is a labor economist and nationally recognized expert in retirement security. She is the Bernard L. and Irene Schwartz Professor of Economics at The New School for Social Research, director of the Schwartz Center for Economic Policy Analysis (SCEPA), and also directs The New School's Retirement Equity Lab (ReLab). Ghilarducci is a court-appointed trustee for the $54 billion medical trust plans for United Auto Worker retirees from GM, Ford, and Chrysler, and for United Steelworkers retirees from Goodyear. She was formerly a trustee for the Indiana Public Employee Retirement Fund, a member of the advisory board for the Pension Benefit Guarantee Corporation, and a corporate director for the Young Women's Resource Center.

 HAMILTON (TONY) E. JAMES is president and chief operating officer of Blackstone. He is a director of Costco Wholesale Corporation and has served on a number of other corporate boards. Mr. James is a commissioner of the Port

Authority of New York and New Jersey as well as serving as a trustee of The Metropolitan Museum of Art and as a member of the boards of trustees of the Mount Sinai Health System and the Center for American Progress. He is also vice chairman of Trout Unlimited's Coldwater Conservation Fund, a trustee of Woods Hole Oceanographic Institute, and a trustee of the Wildlife Conservation Society. He serves on the advisory board of the Montana Land Reliance and is chairman emeritus of the board of trustees of American Ballet Theatre. He is also a former member of the President's Export Council, Subcommittee on Technology and Competitiveness.

Made in the USA
Middletown, DE
16 October 2016